MW00723732

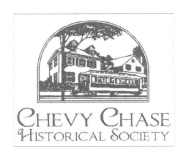

THE
PLACENAMES
OF
CHEVY CHASE, MARYLAND

BEING AN ANECDOTAL STROLL
THROUGH THE
CENTURIES AND NEIGHBORHOODS
OF CHEVY CHASE...

back channel press
portsmouth, new hampshire

The Placenames of Chevy Chase, Maryland
Copyright © 2011 by The Chevy Chase Historical Society
ISBN 13: 978-1-934582-223-7
ISBN 10: 1-934582-23-9

THE CHEVY CHASE HISTORICAL SOCIETY
P.O. Box 15145
Chevy Chase, Maryland 20825
www.chevychasehistory.org

Design and layout by Nancy Grossman
Back Channel Press
www.backchannelpress.com

Printed in the United States of America
Library of Congress PCN 2009912396

Table of Contents

Introduction

The Chevy Chase Historical Society is proud to present this history of Chevy Chase, Maryland. Chevy Chase has the distinction of being one of the first planned suburbs in the United States, founded in 1892 by Francis G. Newlands. This book traces the history of a unique real estate development adjacent to the nation's capital.

Thanks to a grandmother who nicknamed her grandson "Chevy Chase," the place name has been spread wherever comedy movies are shown, much to the surprise of the residents of Chevy Chase. These residents live in properties developed by the Chevy Chase Land Company since 1892. The United States Postal Service includes a broader swath of householders in its zip code of 20815, but this guidebook limits itself to the Land Company's purchases and annexations in Maryland.

The mission of the Chevy Chase Historical Society is to collect, record, interpret and share materials relating to the history of Chevy Chase, Maryland, one of America's first streetcar suburbs. The organization provides resources for historical research and sponsors a variety of programs and activities to foster knowledge and appreciation of the community's history. The Chevy Chase Historical Society embarked on this project in order to share its extensive collection of historical data, photographs, maps and oral histories with an audience beyond its membership. Careful research in the Society's archives provided the material for the text. Its collection of over 7,000 photographs and maps yielded the illustrations. The result is a glimpse into the past and a view of the present to satisfy your curiosity and jog your memory. It is hoped it will also encourage readers to contribute additional recollections for the next edition.

CHAPTER 1

EARLY SETTLERS

Clean Drinking was the home of Nicholas Jones, a descendant of early settlers.

An early document from 1772 established that Montgomery County was carved out of Frederick County.

Maryland was named for Henrietta Maria, the French wife of Charles I of England. In 1629 the king gave George Calvert (Lord Baltimore) a gift of land in the New World and Calvert named the colony Maryland for Queen Mary, the English version of her name.

Montgomery County was carved out of Frederick County in 1776 and named for the patriot Major General Richard Montgomery. (Prior to that time counties were named for British royalty.) Born in Ireland, Montgomery was commissioned in the British army, fought in Quebec for the British against the French, emigrated to New York in 1772, took command of American forces in Quebec against the British and was killed on December 31, 1775, in the ill-fated campaign. He was one of the first heroes of the Revolutionary War.

Chevy Chase recalls the Battle of Chevy Chase in 1388, a border skirmish (or *chevauchee* as the Scots called it) between English Lord Percy and Earl Douglas of Scotland in the Cheviot Hills. With their hunting grounds at stake, the fighting was fierce. Douglas was killed and Henry Percy (Shakespeare's Hotspur) was taken prisoner.

The fury of the Chevy Chase battle is shown in an early engraving.

The battle was commemorated in the plaster frieze for a room in the Cornish castle at St. Michael's Mount, England.

"The Ballad of Chevy Chase," left, was put to the music of a Northumbrian pipe tune in the 19th century. Courtesy of Kay Jones.

The words were reworked by the poet Shelley and another version was composed by Sir Walter Scott, below. Chester's Concert Pieces, vol. 1.

This particular battle was celebrated in song, story and embellishment for hundreds of years. In 1641 a plasterwork frieze depicting it was installed in the monks' refectory when St. Michel's Mount in Cornwall was remodeled as a private house. In ballad form, English and Scottish versions of *The Battle of Chevy Chase* were popular in the 18th and 19th centuries.

Colonel Joseph Belt chose **Cheivy Chace** as the name for his land grant from a later Lord Baltimore in 1725. A century and a half later, Belt's land was the largest tract purchased for Francis Newlands' new sub-

A 19th century oak sideboard was carved to illustrate the English version of the battle of Chevy Chase, now in private hands.

urb, and Newlands adopted the name for his community.

The early development of Lord Baltimore's Maryland colony took place in the south, and it was only gradually that settlers ventured away from the two navigable rivers, the **Potomac** and the **Patuxent,** into the forested interior which had long been the hunting ground of the Indians.

Maryland's indigenous population, the Piscataway Indians, were a peaceful tribe who had welcomed the Europeans as allies against the more bellicose Susquehannock and Seneca to the north. Inevitably disease and the constant encroachment of the white settlers took their toll on the Native Americans, and by the middle of the 18th century most of the remaining Piscataway had withdrawn into Pennsylvania.

Lord Baltimore obtained a unique charter from King Charles which gave him almost total power over his new dominions. As Proprietor, Baltimore and his heirs enjoyed perpetual possession of all the land and water within the bounds of Maryland.

❖

A settler could not purchase land, but instead was issued a warrant to survey the land he wanted. When the survey was approved by the land registry, he obtained a patent to prove his claim. The settler then had to pay an annual "quit rent" to the Proprietor for the use of the land. It could be passed to his heirs, or sold to another party, but should he die without issue the land was "escheated," or returned to the Proprietor. This archaic system of land use would not change until the American Revolution permanently ousted the proprietary government.

In the late 17th century and early 18th century five large grants were patented in the area that became **Chevy Chase: Clean Drinking, Charles and Thomas, Labyrinth, Cloun Close** and **Cheivy Chace.**

Clean Drinking, 1,400 acres acquired from Major William Dent by John Courts in 1688, was one of the earliest grants and was situated at the northern end of Chevy Chase. John Courts raised tobacco, the cash crop of the colony, on Clean Drinking, probably named for its clear spring waters. Not until about 1750 was the so-called manor house raised by Charles Jones who married Courts' granddaughter. Built of wood, as were most of the early plantation houses, it had three chimneys and a kitchen located in a separate building due to the danger from fire.

The Clean Drinking spring still flows, but Nicholas Jones and his house are gone.

In the latter part of the 18th century eight members of the Jones family lived there and farmed the land. They had a mill on **Rock Creek** which gave its name to **Jones Mill Road.** The family is also recalled with **Jones Bridge Road,** but no trace of the mill or bridge remains. When the house was abandoned in the early 20th century, graves from the family burial ground behind the house were moved to Rock Creek Cemetery.

Shortly after Charles Jones built his house, he sold 700 acres on the west side of his grant to Captain Arthur Lee, who in turn conveyed the land to a Major Yates. In 1762 the Reverend Alexander Williams, curate of the **Prince George's Parish,** bought the land and laid out the plans for a magnificent Georgian house. It took some time to complete, and

Hayes, now called Hayes Manor, still stands on Manor Drive.

it was about 1766 that Reverend Williams moved into **Hayes** with his 16-year-old bride. According to tradition, he named the house for the home of William Pitt, the 18th-century English statesman. (Hayes is an alternate spelling for *haies,* French for "hedges.") Hayes was owned for many years by the Dunlop family. The east wing was added in 1894 by George Dunlop, and his son built the west wing in 1908. The house passed through several ownerships before being purchased by the **Howard Hughes Medical Institute** in 2002. The plantation, less the house and 25 acres, was sold to William Stewart, Newlands' partner, in the 1890s as part of the property deeded by the Chevy Chase Land Company to **Columbia Country Club** for its golf course.

By the time Nicolas Jones, the last member of the Clean Drinking family, died in 1911, the original farm was much reduced, and only 23 acres of land were left. Jones' heirs

❖

agreed to have the property sold at public auction. It was offered three times in the following four years, but the highest bid of $8,950 was rejected by the trustees. During this time the house became derelict and in 1916 it was bought by retired Navy Captain Chester Wells.

The Wellses had been acquiring portions of the old estate since 1910, and in 1927 they built a Georgian Revival mansion called **Woodend** on the top of the hill above Jones Mill Road. The house was designed by John Russell Pope, and was modeled after Marion Wells' home outside Sydney, Australia.

In 1967 Mrs. Wells willed 40 acres of this property to the Audubon Naturalist Society for a wildlife sanctuary. The acreage to the rear of the mansion was sold to a developer for residential housing on what is now **Brierly Road.** A portion of the estate south of Jones Mill Road was deeded to **Rock Creek Park.** The land at the corner of Jones Mill Road and Jones Bridge Road, near the Clean Drinking manor house site, is now the site of the Manor Care Health Facility.

A few years after Courts patented Clean Drinking, three more grants were patented to the south and west that would play a part in the development of Chevy Chase. **Cloun Close** was patented in 1713-1714; **Charles and Thomas** in 1716; and **Labyrinth** in 1732. Pieces of these grants were cobbled together to form today's Chevy Chase.

Most of the Charles and Thomas grant lay west of what is now **Connecticut Avenue** and eventually became part of Chevy Chase **Section 4.** Labyrinth bordered it on the east, and joined part of Charles and Thomas to become **Section 3.** Another piece of Labyrinth along with part of Cloun Close comprises **Martin's Additions.** There is little early history on the development of these grants.

In 1716 William Ray bought the entire 419-acre Charles and Thomas grant from the original owners and a few years later passed it on to his sons and a grandson.

❖

The property was sold several times before 219 acres of it were purchased by John Cartwright, who also bought 125 acres of Labyrinth. In the 1750s Cartwright combined the parcels into what was to become the plantation of **No Gain.** He kept the land for 10 years and may have built the log cabin that still stands on the property.

In 1767 Cartwright sold the land. It was subsequently divided, to be pieced together again by Zachariah Maccubbin in 1780. Maccubbin, a tobacco planter, kept the land for 25 years, and it was he who named it No Gain. By 1789 he built a farmhouse for his family.

A century later the Maccubbin house had deteriorated, and the property had become known as **Brooke Farm.** In the 1920s additions were made to the old farmhouse, and it reassumed its name of No Gain. The origin of No Gain's name is unclear. It may have come from the difficulty in

The log cabin at No Gain could have served as a home for Cartwright, and as an early home for Maccubbin. Remodeled, it is today an elegant suburban house.

The core of the No Gain house remains on Thornapple Street.

working the farm's poor soil. More likely, it reflected owner Maccubbin's disappointment when a 1786 survey of his land showed it contained fewer acres than previously thought.

The last of the grants was the one which gave Chevy Chase, Maryland, its name. In 1725 Colonel Joseph Belt patented 560 acres which he called Cheivy Chace. Belt was a colonel in the county militia, charged with defending the outlying settlements. He probably fought under the famous Ninian Beall who commanded the militia for many years. Belt became Beall's son-in-law when Belt married Hester, one of Ninian's daughters.

Belt's life is commem-orated on a marker at Chevy Chase Circle.

Belt patented over a dozen tracts, but chose to live in Cheivy Chace, now spelled Chevy Chase. His grant extended south into the **District of Columbia**, and his house stood on the District side of the line. Belt gave his name to **Belt Road,** one of the few early roads to lead north from the city. It survives in only a few short blocks near 41st Street on the west side of Connecticut Avenue. As it enters Maryland, the street becomes **Brookeville Road** which ran to the town of **Brookeville** in eastern Montgomery County. This book retains the original spelling for the road, but today State road signs omit the first "e".

It was probably Belt's son Thomas who built a farmhouse on part of their land north of today's **Chevy Chase Circle.** In 1814 Abraham Bradley purchased the farmhouse and its surrounding 218 acres, and the land became known as the **Bradley Farm.** The farm remained in the Bradley family for many years, connected to what is now **Wisconsin Avenue** by a dirt road known as **Bradley Lane.** In 1894 over nine acres were leased from its owners by the Chevy Chase Land Company to become the site of the **Chevy Chase Club.**

By the middle of the 19th century smaller farms were being carved out of the original grants. Between 1875 and 1883, a portion of No Gain was sold to John M. C. Williams. He acquired more than 122 acres and had one of the most

The sketch above of the Bradley farmhouse was made by architect William Rich Hutton, in 1844. Courtesy of Peabody Room, Georgetown Branch, District of Columbia Public Library.

extensive holdings in Chevy Chase when Francis G. Newlands began buying land in the area.

Williams concentrated on farming at first, building a large barn while he lived in a small, temporary house. His permanent home was built near Brookeville Road in 1887 for his bride, Eliza Renshaw. Williams also built several houses for family members who formed a small local community.

The dirt road that led from Brookeville Road to his barn and outbuildings became **Williams Lane.** It was not cut through to Connecticut Avenue until 1913 and did not

❖

become a dedicated street until 1923. In 1910, after John Williams died, Edward M. Jones bought 11.5 acres from Williams' estate and platted a small subdivision that a few years later became part of the newly-formed **Section 5.**

Another early farm belonged to the Cummings family. James and Patrick Cummings had emigrated from Ireland in about 1836. They bought 100 acres and lived together in what was described as a rather primitive house. When James married Mary Ellen Wall, the property was divided, and James took 50 acres along Brookeville Road. His brother kept the remaining 50 acres which extended down into what is now **Chevy Chase, D.C.**

This Williams Lane house built for Eliza Renshaw remained in the Williams family until 1928.

James and Mary had seven children. When James died, his widow decided to build a better home. She sold off 20 acres of forest to the east and built a fine house on **Cummings Lane** called **Pleasant Grove.** The acreage sold to pay for Pleasant Grove eventually became part of **Rollingwood.**

When James's son, Andrew Jackson Cummings, known as **Cy,** married Zelpha Contner, he and his wife and three of his sisters lived in the old farmhouse. Cy was an avid fox hunter and kept a pack of hounds on the property until 1933. His interest in race horses led to his serving as president of the Laurel Race Track. The family farmed their land and kept chickens, ducks, geese, turkeys, pigs, goats and at least one cow. Three generations of the family were to live in the house before the land was developed into **Chevy Chase Manor.**

❖

The 50 acres that Patrick Cummings had acquired in the division with his brother were to the south and east of the Cummings farm. His niece Edith kept house for him, and when Patrick died, he left his farm to her.

Edith's husband George A. Wise started Wise Dairy with his brother Joseph in 1905. The company became known as Wise Bros. Chevy Chase Farm Dairy, with offices in **Georgetown.** Later, with branch offices, it was sold to Chestnut Farms Dairy in the 1930s; all that remained of the Wise name was their brand of mayonnaise.

Cy Cummings, photographed here in the 1920s with his horses, hounds and family, lived on Cummings Lane.

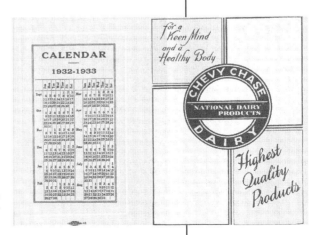

This advertisement for Chevy Chase Dairy was used as a book cover for school children in 1932-1933.

A small parcel of 15 acres from the Belt grant of Chevy Chase was bought by Ottmar Sonnemann. It was just north of the intersection of **Broad Branch Road** and Brookeville Road.

Sonnemann was born in 1824 in Germany, where he studied civil engineering and architecture, receiving a degree from the University of Leipzig. With his brother Frederick he emigrated to the United States in 1849, and the two men operated a dairy in **Tenallytown** (now known as Tenleytown) in the District.

Ottmar met his wife, Rebecca Cox, in Wheeling, West Virginia while working as an engineer. When they settled on 15 acres in Chevy Chase, he continued to work as an engineer. Under General Montgomery C. Meigs he spent a number of years rebuilding the Capitol dome and later was credited with work on the Library of Congress and the **Cabin John Bridge.** Ottmar died in 1904, leaving Rebecca and 10 children. Those children would take prominent roles in the development of Chevy Chase.

Ottmar Sonnemann was a far-thinking patriarch whose property helped support his descendants.

Early residents from Ireland and Germany like the Cummings and the Sonnemanns were joined by Francis Newlands, a Scot. His father was from Edinburgh and his mother from Perth. How much the Scottish connection influenced Newlands in naming his suburb is unknown. But, when he bought the land in 1890, the largest parcel came from Belt's grant, with the Scots-English name of Chevy Chase. It was an additional incentive for Newlands to choose the name.

CHAPTER 2

A PLANNED SUBURB

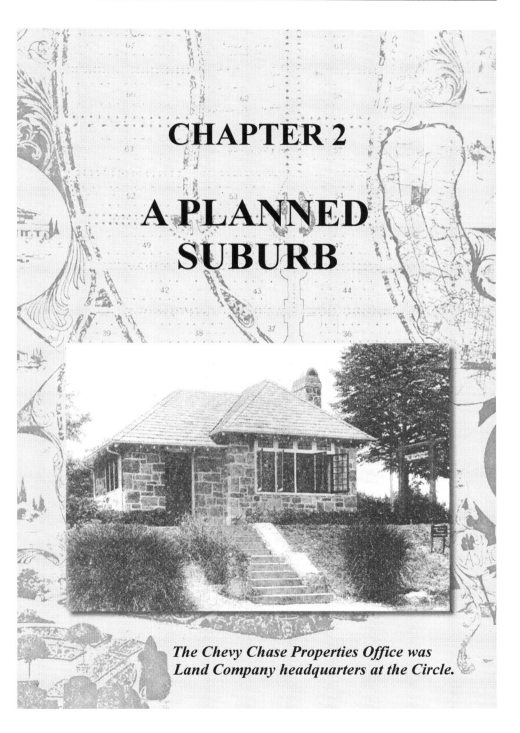

The Chevy Chase Properties Office was Land Company headquarters at the Circle.

Chevy Chase was in great part the creation of one man, Francis G. Newlands. In the late 19th century, the idea of living away from one's place of employment resulted in the

development of suburbs around the country. Newlands set out to transform a large area of what had been rolling farmland into a carefully planned community. It was several miles beyond the boundary of the nation's capital, which meant that a trolley system had to be built to connect it to the city.

Newlands acquired the Rock Creek Railway to be the link, and formed the Chevy Chase Land Company in 1890 to purchase land for the right-of-way. Senator William M. Stewart of Nevada, a longtime associate in Congressional and legal matters, was his chief partner in the initiative.

Francis G. Newlands and his Land Company partners came to be known as the "California Syndicate" because of their connection to William Sharon and others who were based in San Francisco.

The **National Zoological Park,** designed by Frederick Law Olmsted, was moved to a portion of the newly established **Rock Creek Park**. Both in its location, alongside the future **Connecticut Avenue** and in its design by the Olmsted Brothers, Rock Creek Park was a natural barrier to residential development east of Connecticut Avenue.

Newlands was an active promoter of Rock Creek Park and was able to purchase the controlling shares in the Rock Creek Railway. An Act of Congress established the Zoo as an extension of the Smithsonian's natural history exhibits, but meager appropriations from Congress curtailed the scientific plans for the zoo. The electric trolley line made it possible for the public to enjoy the zoo and to convey future residents further along Connecticut Avenue.

Francis Griffith Newlands was born in **Natchez, Mississippi** in 1848. The family soon moved to **Quincy, Illinois.**

After the death of his father in 1851, his mother remarried and the family moved to Washington, D.C., a city that was to play a large role in Newlands' life. He entered Yale University at 16 but had to drop out for lack of funds and returned to Washington, D.C. He took a job at the post office and studied law at the Columbian Law School (now George Washington University).

After becoming a lawyer, in 1870 Newlands went west like many ambitious young men of his time, set up practice in **San Francisco** and soon represented a number of wealthy clients. Among them was Senator William Sharon of **Nevada**, who in the 1870s made his fortune from the **Comstock Lode**, one of the greatest single mineral strikes in history.

In 1873 Newlands married Clara Adelaide, one of Sharon's daughters. They had three daughters and one son. Clara and her son died in 1882, and her father died three years later.
Newlands married Edith McAllister in 1888, but no children survived from that marriage. A short time later, the family moved to a new

Newlands married Clara Adelaide, the daughter of his client William Sharon of San Francisco. Both this photo and that below right courtesy of Eleanor Ford.

Edith McAllister was Newlands' second wife and stepmother to his three daughters.

During his Congressional years, 1892-1917, the official Nevada residence for Newlands was 7 Elm Court, Reno, Nevada. The house was later enclosed in a development called Newlands Heights.

house on the **Truckee River** near **Reno,** Nevada. Although he always maintained a home in the Washington area, Reno became his official residence when he was elected to the U. S. House of Representatives for Nevada in 1892, and in 1902, as one of Nevada's senators. Representing arid parts of the western United States, Newlands was particularly interested in water conservation and utilization. He served on many committees, chaired several, and was responsible for at least three major pieces of legislation.

William M. Stewart was Newlands' Land Company partner, based on a friendship begun in San Francisco and Virginia City, Nevada. They split over federal funding for reclamation projects.

When Sharon died in 1885, Newlands received a percentage of the estate and became a very rich man. As trustee, he found that among the assets was property in the Dupont Circle area of Washington, D.C. In 1887 Newlands decided to sell the lots and use the proceeds to tackle an ambitious project of his own. Senator William Stewart bought land from the Sharon estate and transferred it to the Land Company in exchange for stock.

At that time the city boundary was today's **Florida Avenue**, then called **Boundary Street,** and the area that Newlands and Stewart planned to develop was almost five miles farther to the north in a sparsely settled area of Montgomery County. As his agents purchased parcels along the projected extension of Connecticut Avenue, Newlands transferred a total of 1,713 acres to the Land Company.

The new Rock Creek Railway would link the new suburb to the Capital city, but constructing the rail line was an immense project. The Land Company was responsible for

A trolley, above, is shown here in 1912 crossing the new trestle bridge spanning Rock Creek Valley at Calvert Street.

extending Connecticut Avenue, building the roads and bridging the ravines that were crossed.

Trestle bridges required by the railway charter were constructed over Rock Creek at **Calvert Street** and **Klingle Valley**. The line ran parallel to Rock Creek Park and the Zoo and at Chevy Chase Circle angled due north to **Chevy Chase Lake** in Maryland.

An iron railing from the Calvert Street bridge is preserved as a fence on Quincy Street, salvaged in 1937 when the bridge was rebuilt.

The Rock Creek Railway line opened on September 18, 1892, and the following year was extended along **U Street** east to **7th Street.** The railway's car barns

The Rock Creek Railway terminus, in 1892, included the power house and refreshment kiosk to serve the trolley and the B & O Railroad cars. Courtesy of Leroy O. King.

The car barn, above, was part of the terminus of the Rock Creek Railway at Chevy Chase Lake. Courtesy of Leroy O. King.

General A. J. Warner was the builder and first superintendent of the Rock Creek Railway.

and power house were located at the terminus at Chevy Chase Lake. The lake, created by damming **Coquelin Run,** was on the east side of Connecticut Avenue near the current Chevy Chase Lake Drive, and supplied the water for the steam to make electricity to run the railway.

In front of the powerhouse was a huge car barn that would shelter cars on five tracks, two with pits for servicing and repairs. On the west side of the Avenue, housing was provided for the motormen, conductors and their families, two families to a cottage, with space for little gardens in the rear.

Louis Robertson, a long-time resident of Chevy Chase, described the trolley route:

The outbound streetcars were labeled Chevy Chase Lake, so they went all the way to the Lake, something like a mile north of us. The inbound streetcars were labeled Seventh Street Wharves, and they went down Connecticut Avenue approximately to the Connecticut Avenue bridge, now known as the Taft Bridge, and then turned left on Calvert Street and crossed the Calvert Street Bridge [now known as the Duke Ellington Bridge]. The cars would stop and change from an overhead trolley (wire) to an underground (wire) and then they proceeded on Calvert Street to 18th Street and turned right on 18th Street and went down U Street, where they turned for a long run to the 7th Street Wharves. We would get on, in the early days, at the rear door and pay a fare to a conductor and walk to a seat in the car, and when we exited, it would usually be at the front door.

The trolley and railroad passengers shared a waiting room and the first telephone at Chevy Chase Lake. Later the depot was moved to Frederick County for private use.

The Chevy Chase Land Company purchased land as far north as what is now Jones Bridge Road. The Metropolitan Branch of the Baltimore and Ohio Railroad, in an arrangement with the Metropolitan Southern Railway Company, stopped at Chevy Chase Lake at Connecticut Avenue. In 1910 Thomas Perry, with Newlands' encouragement, set up a business by the railroad siding. Perry was a coal merchant in Kensington, but at the Lake he added hardware and building supplies.

Coal was delivered for the Land Company's power plant and building supplies for trolley line, street maintenance and house construction. "Kit houses," chosen from Aladdin and Sears Roebuck catalogs, were also off-loaded. This cluster of commercial and trolley service buildings defined the northern border of the Chevy Chase Land Company holdings and the Land Company oversight of residential development.

❖

While the Rock Creek Railway was being constructed, Francis Newlands spent much of the early 1890s completing a suburb of San Francisco. **Burlingame Park** was situated on already-acquired land between the **El Camino Real** and the Southern Pacific Railroad tracks, making the development accessible for the planned summer cottages and clubhouse, secured by funds from Sharon's estate.

As he would later do for Chevy Chase, Newlands hired well-known architects and engineers to develop a street plan, design the landscape and provide services for the model cottages. Space for horse racing, hunting, shooting, fishing, lawn tennis and croquet was provided, and food services came from Sharon's Palace Hotel in San Francisco. By 1895 Newlands and his Occidental Land Company had severed connections with the Burlingame Country Club, and he turned his entire attention to Chevy Chase.

After living many years at the Palace Hotel in San Francisco and then in Nevada, Newlands' family acquired 9 Chevy Chase Circle in the mid 1890s. In 1898, at his wife's urging, the family moved to **Cleveland Park** in the District, taking over Woodley, now the Maret School.

In 1909 the house on the Circle was bought by William Corby and remodeled by Arthur Heaton in the Tudor Revival style. William and his brother Carl owned Corby Baking Company. Carl's mansion was **Strathmore** on the **Rockville Pike.**

A domestic water supply was an essential part of Newlands' plan for Chevy Chase. David Howell was selected as the lead engineer. On high ground at **Rosemary Circle**

Newlands' house, much altered, became the William Corby family home.

❖

the Land Company built a 130-foot water storage tower and standpipe in 1893.

A nearby pumping station moved water from the numerous artesian wells in the area. From this source residents were supplied with "pure, clear" water at reliable pressure and at a cost below city prices. With its 300,000-gallon capacity, it continued to supply some residents from 1918 until 1934, when the county could supply all water and sewerage services through the Washington Suburban Sanitary Commission (WSSC).

As the first planning agency, WSSC designed the location of the highways, streets and subdivisions that would be compatible with county-wide sewer and water lines. As old lines were realigned and rebuilt and new lines dug and connected, a method of assessment and a new rate schedule were put in place. Chevy Chase residents had taken pride in their water but recognized and accepted the benefits from the WSSC supply. This meant the end of the usefulness of the water tower at Rosemary Circle.

By the time the tower was dismantled in 1934, many neighborhood children had made the scary ascent. Gus Winnemore relived the escapade:

The Rosemary Circle water tower, photographed here in 1913. Originally serving Section 2 homes, it was situated on a rise in Section 4. The reservoir and pumping station were in the hollow at Valley Place and Beechwood Drive.

Although well above ground, one could get to the stairway, and from there on it was just a question of one's nerves as to how far up the tower he/she could go. The stairs spiraled the tower about two and a half times to reach the top, and the last little bit the stairs were steeper to meet the circular walkway round the top, so these steps were often made on hands and knees to reach it. Then after a spell to recover one could grab the handrail and [stand] up, and see the countryside – a spectacular view in all directions.

❖

Francis Newlands knew the value of meticulous planning. Thomas J. Fisher and Company, a real estate and mortgage banking firm, was chosen as the sole leasing agent by the Land Company. Each day Congress was in session, Newlands stopped at the Fisher office to be briefed on the Land Company's business. The Union Trust Company handled the assets of the Land Company and assisted in financing its ventures. It also provided the headquarters and some of the officers for the Railway, the Land Company and the Fisher Company.

Nathan Barrett, landscape architect, indicated street alignments and recommended plantings. Courtesy of Judy Robinson.

This sales brochure "Chevy Chase for Homes" advertised architectural diversity and variety.

❖

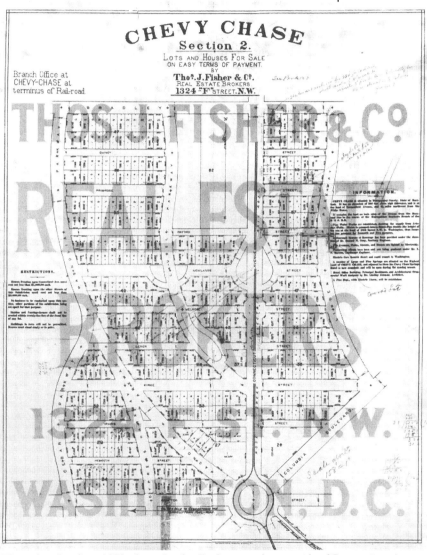

This sales plat, from 1892, shows Linden Parkway on the east side of Connecticut Avenue, a road which was never developed.

❖

In keeping with the reach of his vision, Newlands obtained the services of prominent architect Lindley Johnson of Philadelphia to design the first Chevy Chase houses. Leon Dessez was appointed supervising architect for their construction. Dessez already had made a reputation with the Army Corps of Engineers for "building safety." In 1908 he would help the D.C. Commissioners revise Washington's building code. Landscape architect Nathan Barrett's plan for Chevy Chase proposed double rows of shade trees, ornamental shrubs and hedges of boxwood to define walkways.

Barrett was a self-taught landscape architect with a national practice as a disciple of the noted Frederick Law Olmsted and Andrew Jackson Downing and his master plan gave Chevy Chase the park-like appearance that it retains to this day. Samuel Gray, a nationally known sanitary engineer, was hired to handle the construction of the sewerage system, the water lines and storm drains. Gray's design for Providence, Rhode Island, was one of the most innovative systems in the United States.

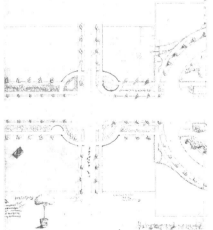

In this 1892 plan for Connecticut Avenue the first order for plant material included 14 chestnut trees, 16 beeches and 300 boxwoods.

Chevy Chase Land Company guidelines were clear. Houses fronting on Connecticut Avenue must cost at least $5,000; on the side streets, $3,000.

Commercial buildings were not allowed. All houses must be single family homes. There were to be no row houses or apartments. No racial or religious covenants appear in the early deeds, but economic restrictions would have limited prospective buyers.

Stables and carriage houses were not to be erected within 25 feet of the front line of the lot, and this presumably also applied to chicken coops, dog houses, cowsheds, tool sheds and greenhouses. Like their contemporaries in other suburbs, residents were encouraged to have vegetable

❖

gardens in their back yards and to raise a few hens. Fruit trees and berry bushes were often an inheritance from the farms that had occupied the landscape.

Well-drained, cement-floored cellars were advertised elsewhere, but a flooded basement was the one hazard of living in spring-fed Chevy Chase.

Many of the street names derive from Barrett's selection of plantings: **Magnolia, Elm, Maple, Beech, Aspen, Oak, Blackthorn, Pine, Willow, Linden, Cedar, Laurel, Cypress** and **Sycamore**.

At first the Land Company favored the names of American cities (to be arranged alphabetically south to north) but before their usage was established these were replaced with names having English associations like **Lenox, Oxford, Kirke** and **Melrose;** or **Hesketh** for Newlands' British brother-in-law Sir George Fermor-Hesketh (husband of Flora Sharon). Another street, **Quincy,** recalls Newlands' step-father's town in **Illinois**, and **Stanford**, the California University that held shares in the Land Company.

There was also to be a Newlands Circle, but it never materialized and survives as **Newlands Crescent**, a pocket park. *In Chevy Chase, nature and man have combined their efforts with charming results,* said an advertisement for Newlands' suburb.

CHAPTER 3

A STREETCAR TO HOME

Passengers waited for the trolley at the Capital Traction Station at Chevy Chase, circa 1900.

❖

The Chevy Chase Land Company's plans projected five adjoining "sections" to be built in chronological sequence on either side of Connecticut Avenue, from the District line north to Jones Bridge Road. The land for **Section 1** was part of the **Belmont Farm.**

Purchased by the Land Company, Section 1 was still being used for fox hunting in 1892 and was later leased to the Bannockburn Club for use as a golf course. When the Bannockburn Club moved to **Cabin John**, the land was leased again to the Kirkside Golf Club and to the English Cricket Club. It was not incorporated into the Land Company for subdivision until 1925. For that reason the first area to be developed was **Section 2.** The plat was filed in November 1892.

Newlands wanted Connecticut Avenue to join Wisconsin Avenue and form a continuous highway from Washington to **Rockville.** When he was unable to purchase a property which was the key piece in the route he had chosen, he realigned Connecticut Avenue from northwest to due north at **Chevy Chase Circle** on land that was available.

A trolley passes a treeless Chevy Chase Circle in 1913. Courtesy of the Montgomery County Historical Society.

❖

The circle was the entrance to the new suburb, a traffic circle similar to those in the L'Enfant plan for the capital city. Lindley Johnson designed an elaborate classical temple for the circle which was never constructed. Early photographs show the circle bare and treeless. Not until 1933 was a fountain, designed by Edward W. Donn, installed and dedicated to the memory of Senator Newlands. It honored him as "the father of waters" for his federal legislation on water reclamation and his planned suburb of Chevy Chase.

The land for Section 2 consisted of 155 acres, much of which was dedicated to roads and parks. Bordered on the south by the District line, it continued north to **Bradley Lane.** The plat shows the eastern boundary as **Linden Parkway,** a projected street that was never realized. Instead, the boundary seems to follow Brookeville Road, sometimes crossing it to the east to include a house or two. At **Primrose Street** a large triangle was carved out for Sonnemann property. The western boundary, which abutted the **Belmont Tract**, was **Cedar Parkway.** The boundaries of the section would be changed

The Quinn brothers played in the middle of the Circle in September 1916. Courtesy of John Deeds.

over the years as adjacent areas were added.

It is generally believed that the first four houses were built by the Land Company for its officers. The large house, number 9 on Chevy Chase Circle, was built either for William Stewart or Francis Newlands. It was designed by architect Lindley Johnson and was later greatly enlarged by architect Arthur B. Heaton. A prairie-style house was built on Connecticut Avenue for Land Company vice-president

❖

The Lodge on Connecticut Avenue was built for Stellwagen in 1892, though architect Leon Dessez moved into the Lodge instead.

The Gates' laboratories, below, are visible in the background of this photograph. It was the largest privately-funded research institution in the nation in its day, a philanthropy of Phoebe Hearst.

Leon Dessez was supervising architect for the Land Co.

❖

Edward Stellwagen, but it was actually occupied by Leon Dessez. The house came to be called The Lodge because for a time it served as lodging for members of the Chevy Chase Club.

A later occupant, Dr. Elmer Gates, was a noted scientist. Behind the house he built laboratories where he conducted experimental research in psychology and psychurgy (the function of the mind). The laboratory buildings were given up around 1908 when Dr. Gates moved to a new home in the city. The Lodge is no longer visible from Connecticut Avenue, because newer houses have been built fronting the street.

The house built for the Land Company treasurer, Howard Nyman, was on the east side of Connecticut Avenue, a prairie-style house demolished in the 1930s. The last of the original houses still in existence is opposite, on the west side of Connecticut Avenue. Built in 1893, it was purchased

Civil engineer Herbert Claude was the Chevy Chase Land Company's on-site representative for many years. Claude's sister Jessie Claude operated the post office for nearly forty years.

by a retired judge whose son, Herbert Claude, was the supervising engineer for the Maryland portion of the Rock Creek Railway. The Chevy Chase post office was located in a room at the northern end of the house until more permanent quarters were found.

The Claude family was the first to occupy this house at the corner of Connecticut Avenue and West Irving St. It served as the Post Office from 1893-1900.

The timing of Chevy Chase's early development turned out to be unfortunate. A serious financial panic struck the country in 1893, and it would be many years before the Land Company paid dividends to its stockholders. By 1897 only 27 houses had been built. Some of these homeowners received loans from the Land Company.

By 1902 there were thirteen Chesapeake & Potomac (C&P) Telephone Co. lines to private houses, and by 1908 Potomac Electric Power Company (PEPCO) was taking over the provision of electricity from the trolley generator at the Lake. In 1922 Georgetown Gas Light Company would extend service beyond Section 2.

The architecture of the early houses was eclectic. The Ord-Jacobs house, a Classical Revival on **West Kirke Street,** was home to two prominent long-time residents. General James C. Ord's daughter Vida Ord Alexander described early life in Chevy Chase Village in her *Recollections*. Later residents were Ephraim and Flora Jacobs. Flora Gill Jacobs was an internationally known expert on doll houses and the owner of a toy and dollhouse museum.

John Weaver and his wife had been living in the Village since 1895, first on Melrose Street and then in a smaller house on Lenox Street. When Mrs. Weaver unexpectedly had twins, they decided they needed a larger home. Mrs. Weaver's brother was young architect Arthur Heaton, who was just beginning his career when they asked him to design their new house on **East Kirke Street** in 1899. The Colonial Revival home Heaton designed for the Weavers was enlarged by Dr. and Mrs. Whitman Cross, when they purchased it in 1923. Dr. Cross was a well-known geologist, and he and his wife were ardent gardeners. They engaged Rose Greely, a pioneering woman landscape designer, to plan their garden and grounds. The Crosses created several new varieties of roses in their garden, and were leaders in the Potomac Rose Society. Niels J. Hansen, their gardener, developed the Chevy Chase Rose in 1939, a crimson climber which is still available today.

Rose Greely's garden design is still visible at the E. Kirke house. Her father, Adolphus Greely, is remembered as the explorer who survived being marooned on an arctic expedition. Courtesy of Mr. and Mr. John Greely.

The lifeline to the city for most Chevy Chase residents was the ever-dependable trolley, which reached the Treasury Department in less than half an hour. It carried the men to work and the children to school. Its freight car obligingly brought groceries ordered from city stores, and delivered them to specified destinations. The conductors knew many of their passengers, and would even return the pet dog of one young resident to its home after the dog accompanied its owner to school. Nearly everyone kept chickens, and a few residents kept horses and carriages. The stables that remain have been converted to garages. One exception is the carriage house of the Weaver-Cross house which has been greatly expanded to become a comfortable home.

The origins of the carriage house of the Weaver-Cross house are disguised by the handsome renovation.

❖

The community of Chevy Chase was still a small one, and its informality encouraged friendly gatherings of all kinds. Vita Ord Alexander describes some simple pleasures:

Deep woods, farm fields and country roads surrounding the village made it a haven for birds, and many residents organized bird walks. Mrs. James Dudley Morgan, always very public spirited, used to take her own children and others, complete with field glasses and bird guides. Walking was indulged in more when the roads were not crowded with cars. Favorite strolls were to Peirce Mill through the Park, to the woods around the water tower to climb the spiral stairway and look at the view, and to Clean Drinking Manor on Jones Mill Road in the spring when the daffodils were blooming and Mr. Jones let his guests pick all they could carry home.

Boys gathered to play ball and marbles in the many vacant lots, and some formed a Gun Club which met on the Dessez property at **Irving Street** and Brookeville Road**.** A large ornamental granite stone once stood at the corner of Irving Street and Connecticut Avenue. This was known as the "loafing stone" and neighbors would meet there to pass the time and share local news. During the summer, church lawn fetes and strawberry festivals were held, lighted by Chinese paper lanterns strung through the trees. All denominations helped organize the events at All-Saints Church and came to boost the sales. The families of the conductors and motormen who lived near Chevy Chase Lake also helped at these affairs.

In 1910 residents of Chevy Chase acquired some important rights from the Maryland State legislature. A new law was passed establishing special taxing districts which would give the residents of Chevy Chase a considerable degree of self-government. This law allowed the various sections to localize the cost of such services as police protection, fire services, street maintenance and garbage collection. Elected governing bodies in these districts still hold public meetings

❖

to discuss local business, and the annual tax rate is always set by the voters themselves. In 1914 Section 2 became a special taxing area. For many years it was known as the Village of Chevy Chase, but it became an incorporated municipality in 1951 and adopted the name **Chevy Chase Village.**

With the rise of self-government, Herbert Claude was no longer needed as a go-between for the Land Company. The Village elected its first and only mayor, William T. S. Curtis, in 1911. One of his early problems was the condition of the local sewers. Walter Tuckerman, who lived in **Bethesda,** had complained that the Chevy Chase sewer field (which ran through **Somerset)**, "stank to high heaven" and had a depressing effect on property values. The state legislature passed a bill in 1916, dealing more with an adequate water supply than with the sewer situation, but it was a start. The Washington Suburban Sanitary Commission (WSSC) was responsible for Montgomery and Prince George's counties, but water for fire protection and safe drinking water were woefully inadequate for the demand.

William T. S. Curtis, the first mayor of Chevy Chase, was chosen the first chairman of the WSSC after negotiating the sewer crisis.

In later years Section 2 changed its governmental organization, appointing a Village Manager instead of a mayor and forming a Board of Managers as the administrative body for the Village. The first Village manager was Edward S. Northrup. He arranged for new brick sidewalks and assessed the condition of the many trees in the Village. At the same time he was attending law school at night, which led to a stellar career as an attorney, majority leader of the State Senate and U.S. District Court judge.

❖

After several years of slow growth, Section 2 began a period of rapid expansion. By 1916 about 145 houses had been built, and almost all the available lots had been sold. House styles varied. The Shingle Style was particularly popular between 1892 and 1910. Stanwood Cobb, a philosopher and internationally known educator, lived in one such house on **Grafton Street.** He began a progressive school called Chevy Chase Country Day School on West Kirke Street, and later moved it to Grafton Street. It was the laboratory for his many books on educational theory. He emphasized

the importance of playgrounds as well as music and arts and crafts. Eventually the Cobb School included all grades and accepted boarders. The curriculum was unusual and some of the classes unconventional. Over the years the enrollment stayed small but steady and the alumni went on to colleges and careers. Cobb published several books on spirituality before he died in 1983 at the age of 101, outliving his school and his wife, Nayan Whitlam Cobb.

Dr. Stanwood Cobb was a distinguished personage in the world of education. Courtesy of Lawrence Heilmann.

Dr. Cobb's Chevy Chase Country Day School, first located on West Kirke Street, was later moved to a house on Grafton Street.

❖

On Connecticut Avenue, between Bradley Lane and Quincy Street is **Dudlea**, one of the most imposing houses in the Village. The Colonial Revival house occupies more than an acre of land. Dr. James Dudley Morgan, a descendant of the Carroll family of Maryland, built the house in 1909 as a summer home. Charles Carroll Morgan, James' son, lived in the house year round, and his family continued to do so until 1970, when they carved out a small lot facing Quincy Street and built a one-story house there, after selling Dudlea.

The porches were later removed from Dudlea. Courtesy of Leroy Morgan.

Dudlea, like other early houses, was located with an entrance on Connecticut Avenue. The trolley passed frequently on weekdays and more frequently on Sundays. The Rock Creek Railway had merged with George Dunlop's Capital Traction Company in 1895, allowing Chevy Chase residents access to the entire city from Chevy Chase Circle for a five cent fare. With a transfer, a passenger could change for Georgetown or the Navy Yard, but thanks to Newlands' concept, there would be plenty of amenities at home. Chevy Chase provided a congenial community and that is what the residents had sought when they settled in the neighborhood.

Looking south, a motorman stands on unpaved Connecticut Avenue in 1910 next to the double trolley rails. The mailboxes for Mechanics Row (also called Watkins Avenue or Brick Row) are to the right of the photo.

CHAPTER 4

BUILDING
A COMMUNITY

*The Chevy Chase Lake power house and
streetcar terminus provided electricity for
the trolleys and the residences.*

❖

Newlands and his business partners were interested in founding more than a new suburban development. They wanted to establish a community. Chevy Chase would need schools, churches and other amenities to draw residents from the city. At that time in Montgomery County there were only one- and two-room school houses scattered across the farmland, and schools in the District were inconveniently distant. In 1898 the Land Company donated its small Fisher Company sales office on Chevy Chase Circle to be used as a school which could accommodate 26 pupils. When this space was outgrown, funds were provided for a new building on the northwest corner of Bradley Lane and Connecticut Avenue just outside the limits of Section 2. This school operated for only five years.

This 1930s photograph shows the Bradley School building which was in operation from 1898 to 1903.

Again the Land Company came forward and donated land for a public school, this time on Connecticut Avenue south of the District line. It opened in 1898. Chevy Chase School provided a fine education for its pupils, under the leadership of the talented and popular principal, Ella Given. It was the school of choice for most students of Chevy Chase for many years, although the decision made by District authorities in 1899 to charge tuition to parents who did not live or work in the city was a handicap to overcome.

❖

Not until 1915, when prominent educator Miss E. V. Brown died, was the school renamed in her honor. That year another Chevy Chase School was established at Rosemary Circle and Valley Place. It was simpler to refer to the District school as E. V. Brown and the county school as Valley View. The neo-classical building that housed the E. V. Brown School was torn down in 1942 to make room for the present-day public library and community center.

Several short-lived private schools were also started in the area. Rose Mactier's was just north of Section 2 on the corner of Bradley Lane and Connecticut Avenue. Miss Mackrill's school was in her home at 3 Grafton Street, and Clothilde Cunningham had

The popularity of Ella Givens, the first principal of E. V. Brown School, helped the school expand.

her Peniel School at Brookeville and E. Lenox Street. Miss Libbey's School in the Village Hall was the most permanent one. It began in 1935 and lasted more than 20 years.

Two of Newlands' daughters, Edith and Janet, married brothers, Charles H. L. Johnston and Dr. William B. Johnston. The sisters led the drive for a Chevy Chase Library through the formation of the Chevy Chase Library Association. They not only planned a library building but also offered to fund the purchase of the books. In 1900 the Land Company donated a sizeable piece of land fronting on Connecticut Avenue and funded the one-story stucco building designed by Arthur Heaton. That structure is today the Village Hall.

The library had an impressive collection of books and was one of the first libraries in Montgomery County. The Ladies Reading Class, which met on East Lenox Street, supported the Village library. (It also supported the library

The Village Hall has been remodeled several times. The Post Office now has its own wing, the police have parking and the interior is reconfigured.

The steel rim of a locomotive wheel, mounted at the south end of the Village Hall, served as a gong to summon volunteers from their homes to fight fires.

in the Chevy Chase Elementary School until the public school system took it over in the 1960s.) The Village library evolved into a recreational center for the community. Meetings, dance classes, benefit shows and parties of all kinds are still held there. Today the Village Hall contains the offices for the Village and continues to be a focal point for community activities.

At one end of the building was a separate entrance for the new post office, moved from the Claude house. A telephone was installed next to the post office. Space was provided for the community police force and for storing the fire-fighting equipment. Since everyone heated with coal furnaces or wood-burning fireplaces, there was constant risk of fire from sooty chimneys. In addition, most houses had wooden shingle roofs, which were easily ignited by flying sparks. The Village had volunteer firefighters, but if a fire spun out of control, the more sophisticated company at Tenallytown came to the rescue with its horse-drawn equipment.

St. John's Episcopal Church had been situated at the corner of **Bradley Lane** and Wisconsin Avenue since 1874. At the request of new residents, in 1897 St. John's rector began to hold services in the same little sales office on Chevy Chase

St. John's Episcopal Church was an established landmark in 1910.

Circle where the first school was housed. In 1901, ground was broken for All Saints Episcopal Church at Chevy Chase Circle on land donated by the Land Company. It was the first church in Chevy Chase, established as a mission church from St. John's. Architects Waddy Wood and Arthur Heaton designed the English-style stone chapel. Between 1921 and 1926 the size of the church was increased by expanding the nave and adding a chancel and sanctuary on the southern end of the new building.

The first Catholic church in Chevy Chase, the Shrine of the Most Blessed Sacrament, was also a mission church, this one sponsored by St. Ann's in Tenallytown. The first mass was held in 1910 in the Village Library. With the backing of Dr. James Morgan and Dr. John Ryan Devereux, the first building was dedicated in 1911. Responding to the steady sale of residential properties, the parish outgrew its simple frame structure and started a school. The cornerstone for the permanent church was laid in 1925, and a short time later a drive was begun for a permanent school. A new building was completed in 1929, and the school has grown and flourished. The Land Company, which had prohibited apartments, allowed a 16-unit apartment building to be built on District land next to the Catholic Church.

The Blessed Sacrament cornerstone was set before a large crowd in 1925. Courtesy of Management of Chevy Chase Apartments.

Blessed Sacrament is on the District side of Western Avenue, just off Chevy Chase Circle.

Preliminary steps have been taken for the potential beatification and canonization of Miss Merrick, who lived on Melrose Street. Courtesy of the Christ Child Society.

The most noted member of this early church was undoubtedly Mary Virginia Merrick. Due to an accident at age 14, Miss Merrick was confined to a wheelchair for the rest of her life. In spite of her handicaps she worked unceasingly to support the needs of poor children in the Washington area. In 1884 she and her friends gathered to sew layettes, and from this small group grew the Christ Child Society which has become a national organization.

Francis Newlands was interested in forming a social club that would attract members from the city. The initial interest for the club was fox hunting. In 1892 the Dumblane Hunt Club, which had been based on Dumblane Farm in Tenally-town, was looking for new quarters. Newlands offered them temporary space on the Belmont Tract, together with a promise to help them find a permanent home. For a brief

❖

time the hunt was referred to both as the Dumblane Hunt and the Chevy Chase Hunt. By 1893, the plans for a club incorporating the hunt had materialized, and Newlands negotiated a lease for the 9.36-acre Bradley Farm then still in private hands.

During the War of 1812 valuable government records were said to be stored at the Bradley farm, which became the home of the Chevy Chase Club.

The farmhouse, which still stood on the property, in all probability had been built sometime before 1760 by the Belt family. The new Club made a large clubroom out of several first floor rooms and built locker rooms on the east end. Stables and kennels were provided for the fox hunters, and the Chevy Chase Hunt was firmly established in its new home. With so much invested in the location, the Board of Governors of the Club decided in 1897 to purchase the property. Samuel Henry described the countryside where they hunted: *With the Club as the base of a vast arc, the domain, dotted by comfortable farmsteads, spread for miles to the east, north and west into gently rolling hills, almost endless fields of pasture and tillable lands, broken by large forests and winding streams. Galloping over the pastures was exceedingly fine, and the fences and stone walls were not beyond the capacity of a tolerably able horse.*

The Hunt met two or three times a week, and the area was still sufficiently rural that the hounds were kept at the

❖

club until 1906. Complaints by the residents about the baying of the hounds led to their being moved to the **Rock Creek Farms** near Kensington, which had been purchased by the Master of the Hunt, Clarence Moore. Almost 90 horses were stabled there, and between two and five packs of hounds. The colorful Master drove to the meets in a red and black four-in-hand coach accompanied by a liveried coachman blowing on a large brass horn.

Clarence Moore was a striking figure in his Master of the Hunt attire.

In 1912 the hunt suffered a sad reverse. Moore went to England to buy more hounds and returned on the ill-fated *Titanic,* which sank with great loss of life. Moore was among those who did not survive. The 24 hounds arrived safely on another ship, but after Moore's death the hunt was never the same and was abandoned four years later.

The Chevy Chase hunt assembled in 1903 near the clubhouse. Courtesy of the Library of Congress.

❖

The new sport of golf rapidly replaced foxhunting in popularity. The regulations for the size of golf courses were still in a state of flux, and early courses consisted of only four to seven holes. In 1895 the Chevy Chase Club laid out a course of six holes, played on both sides of Connecticut Avenue. Village supervisor Morris Hacker was the architect for the course. The golfers were undeterred by the challenge of hitting over the street car line and Connecticut Avenue to reach new holes. When the Club acquired the Dodge Tract in 1908, extending its property to Wisconsin Avenue, a full 18-hole course was laid out.

Tennis courts had been part of the Club from the beginning. In 1910 they were moved to their present location along Bradley Lane. They hosted many famous matches, as Dwight F. Davis, the man for whom the Davis Cup is named, was a member. Later additions were the large swimming pools built on the northern end of the property.

The 1902 golf tournament at Chevy Chase Club was painted by W. T. Smedley.

❖

   In 1962 the Club decided to introduce winter sports for its members. An ice skating rink, platform tennis and a new informal restaurant called the Winter Center were constructed at the southern end of the property. Like many other country clubs, the Chevy Chase Club began by restricting its membership to men, but women guests of male members could participate in tennis, swimming and other activities. Today, of course, women members are welcome and many activities are designed for children.

The newly remodeled Chevy Chase Club retains various historical features.

The carriage house at the Club was originally home to both stables and a garage.

❖

The District of Columbia weekly, *Kate Field's Washington*, editorialized in 1893 that: *Nowhere are improvements in the suburbs of the Capital so apparent as in the direction of Chevy Chase, seven miles away in Maryland. Thanks to the California Syndicate, a beautiful country has been opened to the public, and new rides and drives galore add to the delights of a winter at the Capital. A large hotel has been put up and charming cottages already dot the landscape.*

The trolley stop for the Chevy Chase Club on Connecticut Avenue is as decorative as a similar one that once stood outside the Columbia Country Club.

The Chevy Chase Inn was on Land Company property north of Bradley Lane on the west side of Connecticut Avenue. Near some natural springs, it had previously been called the Chevy Chase Springs Hotel. The original building was designed by Lindley Johnson in 1892 and opened under the management of the Land Company in 1894, advertising simple meals, dancing and a bowling club. The accessibility provided by the Rock Creek Railway made it an attractive destination for city dwellers during the hot summer months.

❖

The Inn had one successful season, but the attempt to keep it open year round was impractical, so in 1895 the inn was leased for the academic year to a seminary known as the Chevy Chase School for Girls. In 1903 the Land Company sold it to the Chevy Chase College for Young Ladies. Under the direction of Dr. Frederic E. Farrington it functioned as a three-year high school as well as a two-year junior college, and in 1927 as simply the Chevy Chase Junior College. Farrington was followed by Samuel N. Barker, who led the school until his death in 1930. There was room on the 12-acre campus for tennis, basketball and field hockey, and even a seven-hole golf course. In 1940 the school was incorporated as a non-profit institution and developed a cooperative relationship with George Washington University.

After 55 years of operation, the school finally closed in 1950. Its successor, the National 4-H Youth Conference Center, was also attuned to education. The 4-H program began in the late 19th century as an after-school club to improve the lives of young people in rural areas. The 4-Hs stand for Head, Heart, Hands and Health. The organization is supported in part by state land-grant universities and the Extension Service of the United States Department of Agriculture (USDA).

The Chevy Chase Springs Hotel, below, was transformed into the Chevy Chase Junior College by the first quarter of the 20th century. Courtesy of the Chevy Chase Land Company.

Enormously successful, by 1915 there were clubs in almost every state. The National 4-H Foundation was created in 1948 and began to search for a site for its headquarters in the national capital area. The Chevy Chase Junior College campus was ideal, and after rather complicated financial negotiations, a sale was completed in 1951. One aspect of the purchase was an agreement with the Department of Defense to lease the property temporarily for their Office of Research Operations (ORO) during the Korean War.

By 1977 the National 4-H Youth Conference Center needed more space, particularly for housing thousands of overnight visitors annually.

By 1957 the ORO was ready to move on, and the National 4-H Youth Conference Center reclaimed its new home. President Eisenhower cut the ribbon at the opening ceremonies in June 1959. Since then the Center has hosted year-round training programs and conferences for 4-H youth, volunteer leaders and staff. The main building was renovated in 1957 and again, more extensively, in 1977, maintaining only the façade of the original. It is named for the donor, J. C. Penney, the retailer who founded the chain of stores bearing his name. Young 4-H members come from all over the country and from overseas to participate in various citizenship programs, and visit the sites of the nation's capital. The National 4-H Council now maintains the 4-H

Conference Center as a major resource for their members and outside groups. Hundreds of overnight guests can be accommodated and at a dining room sitting. Many thousands visit the conference site each year, without disturbing the neighborhood's tranquility.

In addition to the hotel, in 1894 the Land Company transformed the man-made 3½-acre lake at the terminus of the street railway into an elaborate amusement park. It would be a major inducement to travel to Chevy Chase. Herbert Claude took charge of the park in 1897, along with his railway duties, and continued as park director until 1918. Visitors crossing the wooden bridge over Coquelin Run would see a large pale blue bandstand shaped like a shell, outlined with electric bulbs. Here the Marine Band often played, and John Philip Sousa occasionally appeared to conduct.

As Constance Weaver recalled: *Each year on the 30th of May, a portion of the Marine Band got into an open trolley car and played their gayest tunes all the way out to the Lake, and we all knew that summer was here.*

Red, white and blue lights strung around the lake illuminated it at night. Behind the band stand was a round ring or track for horse and pony rides, or for rides in little carts pulled by goats. Nearby was a wonderful carousel, where winning the gold ring entitled one to a free ride. Local boys like James H. Pugh, who in later life was a State's Attorney and Circuit Court Judge, were hired as staff.

James Pugh remembered: *My duties were to row the boats on the lake, set up bowling pins on the bowling alleys, attend the shooting gallery, attend the boat swings, was the ring boy on the merry-go-round (the carousel), was the hat check boy on the dancing pavilion, along with my four brothers, Mike, Ed, Charlie and Robbie.*

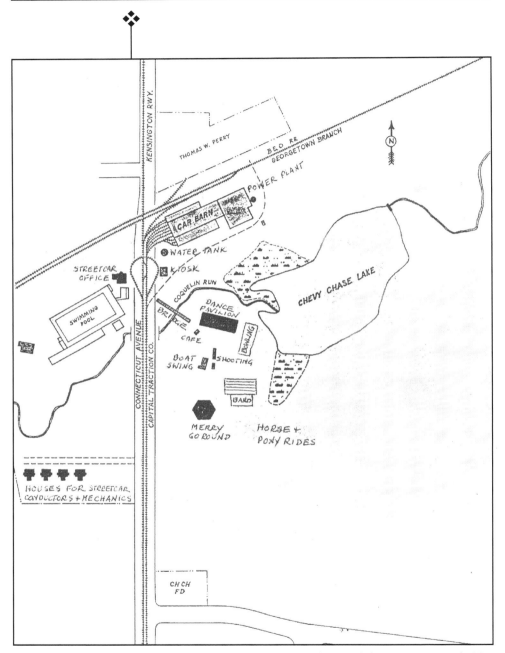

The Lake terminus met the requirements of both the street railway and the amusement park. Map drawn by William Duvall.

The enterprising employees sometimes spent their "free" time catching frogs to provide a delicacy for club menus. The lake was not suitable for swimming (although, oddly enough, diving competitions were occasionally sponsored), but boating and picnicking on the banks were popular for all ages. A cafe also did a brisk business, as did Dan's Hot Dog Stand at the trolley terminus. For only five cents one could see the first movies shown in the Washington area.

James Pugh and friend were at the oars on Chevy Chase Lake in this undated photograph.

The Marine Band concerts were free, and after Sousa's time, Major William Santlemann, who lived in Chevy Chase D.C., was the conductor. Orchestra leader Meyer Davis assumed management of the park after Herbert Claude, and his musicians played there for many years. Famous artists appeared with the orchestra. Kate Smith began her singing career there, Eubie Blake introduced his "Chevy Chase Fox Trot" and Vernon and Irene Castle performed frequently. Into the 1920s the amusement park was an attraction that drew many from the city. By the next decade it was primarily a place to dance, a source of pleasure and recreation until it closed in 1937. The Lake was an important destination, and the neighborhood retains the name to this day.

Chevy Chase Lake

GRAND CONCERT

BY A SECTION OF THE

United   States   Marine   Band

UNDER THE DIRECTION OF WALTER F. SMITH, 2D LEADER

Program

Thursday, June 30, 1904

1. March—"The Seal of Society" . . . . . Burns

2. Overture—"Jolly Robbers" . . . . Suppe

3. Fantasia—"King Dodo" . . . . Luders

4. Intermezzo—"Pagliacci" . . . . . Leoncavallo

5. Waltz—"Beautiful May" . . . . . . Strauss

6. March—"The Spirit of '76" . . . . . Panella

A program from the U.S. Marine Band concert announces its appearance at Chevy Chase Lake.

CHAPTER 5

NEW NEIGHBORS

The historic Stone house, an early landmark, was torn down by mistake.

As Francis Newlands' plan for Chevy Chase began to unfold in the late 19ᵗʰ century, it attracted the attention of landowners north of Section 2 outside of Land Company holdings. Several small subdivisions sprang up which were later folded into Section 4. One of the earliest was **Norwood Heights**, a small community north of Bradley Lane and east of Wisconsin. The Norwood Heights Improvement Company was founded in 1893 by Edwin W. and E. R. Haight of Washington. It was a short-lived venture, a victim of the Panic of 1893, and the company collapsed in 1906.

A centerpiece of Norwood Heights was a preexisting Queen Anne-style house on **Leland Street,** built in 1888. In 1893 it was purchased by William G. Offutt. He and his wife Bettie had five children, one of whom, William, was a successful carpenter and house painter who married Lillian Troth. William served as County Assessor in the 1920s. Also on Leland Street, the northwestern boundary of Norwood Heights, is the Colonial Revival Butterfield House. Benjamin F. and Julia Butterfield often boarded city dwellers who wanted to escape the summer heat. It is now doubled in size with a mirror-image wing.

The Offutt house on Leland Street was occupied by two Offutt sisters until 1965.

On the other edge of Newlands' holdings, four investors – John Frank Ellis, Eugene Clark, Robert E. Earll (R. Edward as he preferred to be called) and Reginald Geare – started **Otterbourne.** Ellis was the one chosen to purchase 14.5 acres of the Williams farm in 1893. **Otterburn** [sic] in Scotland was the site of the battle of Chevy Chase, and Ellis used this name, with the slight change in spelling, in order to stress the link to the larger development in Section 2. The streets were named **Percy** and **Douglas** after the opponents in the battle. Not many houses were built in Otterbourne, and many lots were not improved until after World War I. Baptists, under the leadership of Louise Harding Earll, built a chapel in 1906 at Connecticut Avenue and **Shepherd Street**, but with slow home sales potential members were few.

The first house in the Otterbourne community was the R. Edward Earll house on Thornapple Street, which he sold to William Cummings in 1921 and came to be known as the Cummings house.

Eugene Clark built his house on Underwood Street in 1897 and lived in it for 40 years. It follows the pattern book of New Jersey architect H. Galloway Ten Eyck.

❖

Eventually Otterbourne was absorbed into Section 5 of Chevy Chase. **Percy Street** became **Thornapple Street,** and **Douglas Street** became **Underwood Street** to continue their counterparts on the west side of Connecticut Avenue. But the residents of **Williams Lane** refused to switch from their street-name, which honored a family of residents, to **Virgilia Street.** The streets on the west side of Connecticut continued the alphabetical order begun in the District.

The No Gain estate, which in 1890 comprised 250 acres, was owned by Mary Frances Griffith Anderson Woodward. She died in 1891, just as Section 2 was about to open. Her property became a valuable asset for her heirs. One of them,

Isabella Griffith, subdivided her share into lots along Brookeville Road. The Bradshaw House was on one of the first lots she sold. In 1903 it was called **End Lane** because it was the northern limit of Chevy Chase development until the late 1930s. A tablet on the gatepost designates the house as an Historical Site in the Master Plan for Historic Preservation.

The Simpson property on Brookeville Road was used as the headquarters for their construction company.

Just south of End Lane is the Simpson family house, built by John Simpson for himself. He had purchased the large 3.2-acre lot from the Griffith family in 1905. The property was once the site of barns and other outbuildings connected to his family's thriving construction business. One of John's nephews, Horace Troth, Jr., lived farther south on Brookeville Road and was the official painter for the family business. Another nephew, William Orem Jr., served as the realtor for the company. The three families formed a consortium that built many houses in what would become **Section**

❖

3 and **Martin's Additions**. They also began to intermarry with the Williams family who had retained their property adjacent to Brookeville Road.

The Simpsons helped to build their community and prospered with it. All devout Methodists, members of the Simpson, Troth and Orem families began to meet in the barn of the Williams farm for worship on Sundays. Reverend William Orem came from his church in **Forest Glen** to preach. Soon the group entered into an agreement with the small Baptist Church on Connecticut Avenue to use their building on Sunday evenings, and in 1913 they were able to purchase the little brown chapel for $3,966. The Land Company had donated the land for the Baptist Church, and now it added the choice corner lot to the property. The Methodist Church had strong support from the community and built three successive stone buildings over the years. The present sanctuary, which faces Connecticut Avenue, was consecrated in 1954.

The Baptists built a brown shingle chapel on land that the Land Company donated at Connecticut Avenue and Shepherd Street, with the T. W. Perry house behind.

❖

The Griffiths decided not to develop the remainder of their land themselves. They sold the largest portion to Harry M. Martin. Martin had an insurance and real estate business in Washington, but he lived in Maryland. Martin began subdividing his purchase in 1904 and named it **Harry Martin's Additions to Chevy Chase.** He built four additions, all with more modest purchase prices for the houses than those in Chevy Chase. Martin's Additions has survived as an independent community with its own unique character. Lawrence Troth was given the job of naming the streets. Receiving its taxing status in 1916, in 1985 the development was incorporated under the name of **The Village of Martin's Additions.**

John Mauchly, the inventor of ENIAC, the first digital computer, progenitor of all succeeding computers, was a resident of Martin's Additions.

A reception was held on the occasion of the incorporation of Martin's Additions. Long-time resident and historian Wallace Janssen presented a paper that looked back at the history of the area: *Life was "rugged" in the Village of Martin's Additions in 1916. The streets had barely been cut through – sidewalks, paving, lights, sewers, gas and water,*

❖

all the conveniences which we now take for granted – were only substance of things hoped for. But there was plenty of rain water, and it turned into knee-deep mud.

The residents organized themselves into the Chevy Chase Home Association and produced a solution to their problem. A total of 350 feet of boardwalk was laid across the low places in the fields that separated them from Connecticut Avenue. The residents were assessed $1.50 per family for materials and helped to split the logs for the planks. Janssen added that the path was a great improvement, but it wasn't lighted, and the mud on Brookeville Road was as deep as ever. Folks expecting to come home late carried lanterns and hid them with their rubbers in the bushes near the carline.

Chevy Chase boys with their bicycles at Underwood Street en route to Rock Creek for swimming in the 1920s.

The ladies of Martin's Additions were very active, forming a Community Club that took the lead in raising money for sidewalks. Lawn parties, progressive suppers and food sales raised $350 to build a boardwalk from **Turner Street** to Sonnemann's Store on Brookeville Road.

In the 1920s we all knew each other and knew the occupations of the families, recalled George Winchester Stone. *Though Federal workers perhaps dominated, a general and genuine social mix (save for blacks precluded by property deeds) was evident during the span of three decades – a veterinarian, a Naval Commander, a banker, a grocer, a blacksmith, several attorneys, a high school administrator, several botanical and chemical scientists, a plasterer, a dentist, several eminent doctors, five farmers, two club managers, a prime local politician, a general contractor, several carpenters, and an automobile distributor.*

❖

Most of the federal employees were hired by the Departments of State, Agriculture and Treasury, the General Accounting Office, the Federal Trade Commission, the Public Health Service, the Bureau of Standards and the Bureau of Terrestrial Magnetism. Stone himself was a professor of English Literature at George Washington University.

Stone's aunt, Faith Bradford, was a cataloger for the Library of Congress for many years. In her spare time she designed and furnished a doll house to represent the life of a Chevy Chase family in the year 1905. The furnishings were collected by Miss Bradford over the years, but most of the rugs and window curtains were made by her and her friends. The doll house is complete in every detail, a masterpiece of imagination. Her Doll Family had ten children and each had a named pet. New labor-saving devices, such as a washing machine and a vacuum cleaner, assisted the household staff. A miniature portrait of Miss Bradford's grandfather hangs over the mantel in the dollhouse library. The dollhouse took 50 years to complete and is now on permanent display at the Smithsonian's National Museum of American History.

Faith Bradford's Doll Family enjoyed housekeeping advances before 1905. Courtesy of the Smithsonian's National Museum of American History.

❖

The Esch House in Martin's Additions faced Brookeville Road from the time of Marion Esch's birth in 1915 until she and her husband Neal Potter sold the house in 2007. In 2008 the house was turned 45 degrees on the lot and now faces Raymond Street. Neal Potter was Montgomery County Executive from 1990-1994. He served on the County Council from 1970-1986 and from 1994-1998 for a final term, playing a leading role in legislation to control development and preserve farm land and green spaces. The Montgomery County Conservation Corps was his idea.

The Esch sisters could watch for the occasional automobile on Brookeville Road while sitting on their front porch steps in 1925.

The copious water in Martin's Additions made one block adjacent to the northern end of the development so swampy that no one wanted to build a house there. It was purchased by Dr. Wilbur E. Evans, who developed a small commercial area instead. As it was outside the Land Company holdings, the commercial use was allowed. The first grocery store was called McGoverns, and the first self-service grocery was the Piggly Wiggly. At one time there was a District Grocery

Store (DGS) in the middle of the block and a Safeway at the corner. The DGS disappeared, and the Safeway was eventually replaced by the present Brookville Supermarket. A drugstore was an important addition, and it too has changed ownership several times.

Neighbors depended on local shops long before a recent renovation gave the commercial block on Brookeville Road an attractive face-lift.

It was Harry Martin who led the drive for a Presbyterian Church in Chevy Chase. In 1906 he invited some of his friends and neighbors to come to meet at his house with Dr. George Bailey, the minister of Western Presbyterian in Washington. As a result of this gathering, cottage prayer meeting services were begun in local homes on Sunday afternoons. Dr. Bailey and other ministers from downtown churches came to Chevy Chase in between their own services to conduct them. The popularity of these informal services made public space necessary, and by the next year they had arranged to rent the Chevy Chase Library on Sunday afternoons for $2.50 each week. They also began their first church school in what is now the Village Hall.

In 1908 the members of the informal group asked the Washington City Presbytery for permission to build a church on the District side of Chevy Chase Circle. The Presbytery ruled the church was too far out and that the *neighborhood is unpromising and will never be built up,* but by 1910 a little stucco chapel was under construction by

❖

J. and J. Simpson Brothers, and the first service was held on Christmas Day. The cornerstone for the present fieldstone building facing **Patterson Street** was laid in 1923, with several additions since to accommodate the education department.

Through the years various congregations have been generous with space for community activities such as Boy Scouts, Girl Scouts, nurseries and preschools, foreign language congregations, English as a second language classes and tutoring, and Meals-on-Wheels. All Saints Episcopal has sponsored Boy Scout Troop #52 since 1909. The Fossils, a retired men's club, continues to meet at Chevy Chase United Methodist Church. Churches have sponsored Dutch, Ethiopian, Cambodian, Vietnamese and Polish refugee families. Increasingly the churches have looked to the inner city to offer services and provide meals, funds and volunteers. Choirs and their directors have produced countless concerts of musical distinction.

Because of its location, Chevy Chase Presbyterian came to be known as the Gateway Church.

Before he died, Ottmar Sonnemann divided his farm on **Broad Branch Road**, hoping to help provide for his extensive family. One of Ottmar's sons, Alexander, built some houses for family members in the area, and went on to become a successful architectural engineer. Like his father, he helped build the Library of Congress and the Cabin John Bridge. He designed several houses in Chevy Chase, including the one he built for himself on Grafton Street. Later he would become the chief architect for the **Kenwood** development. Another son and architect was Karl O. Sonnemann. He was supervising architect of the White House under President Truman and a designer of the Reptile House at the National Zoo.

The T. A. Sonnemann and Son store was built on the family property at Quincy Street and Brookeville Road.

Ottmar's oldest son, Theodore, lived in a house on Brookeville Road, and next to his house he built Sonnemann's Store. The family had not sold their land to the Land Company, so Theodore, like Dr. Evans, was able to avoid the Land Company restrictions on commercial property. His horse-drawn wagon delivered groceries directly to houses in the neighborhood in the early

Daily deliveries were made by horse-drawn wagon. The store can be seen in the photo background.

days of Chevy Chase. Theodore created a new subdivision on the family property called **Sections 6 and 7 of Chevy Chase.** His development was absorbed in Chevy Chase Village in 1972 and is now known as **Sonnemann's Additions.**

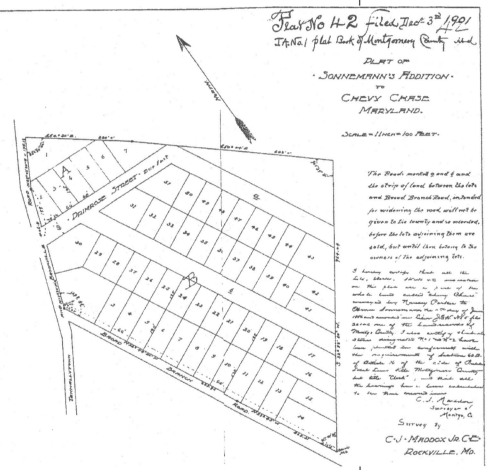

Sonnemann's Additions was platted in 1901.

Norwood Heights eventually became part of Section 4. East of Connecticut Avenue, some of the farms and real estate ventures were added to a small piece already owned by the Land Company to form Section 5 in 1923. The Sonnemanns

❖

maintained their independence even longer, and didn't become absorbed into Chevy Chase Village until the 1970s. Only the Village of Martin's Additions is still a separate subdivision.

The Sonnemanns were neighbors to an ancient, giant white oak on Brookeville Road, struck by lightning in the 1940s. For many years the Garden Club of Chevy Chase has helped with the selection of trees and the plantings in the pocket parks and parklets. Trees first planted by the Land Company have been nurtured and replenished in the century since. Oaks, sycamores and dogwoods have replaced the elms and chestnuts decimated by disease. Red oaks and flowering cherries are preferred for public right-of-ways. Founders of the Camellia Society, like Edith Claude Jarvis, lived in Chevy Chase. She inspired many gardeners to cultivate camellias and camellias continue to be a favored shrub. Similarly, in recent decades new colors and varieties of azaleas brighten gardens, and pink dogwoods have joined the native whites throughout the Sections.

❖

CHAPTER 6

THE PLAN EXPANDS

Smaller lots accommodated smaller houses in Section 3.

Francis Newlands' deep pockets allowed the Land Company to survive the recession that followed the Panic of 1893. After Section 2, the next section to be developed was east of Connecticut Avenue. Platted in 1905, Section 3 was originally part of the No Gain estate. Two years later it was subdivided into smaller lots, and many of the streets were laid out in a grid pattern. It was to be more densely platted than Section 2. A lower minimum cost was set for the houses, which were smaller but no less distinctive. Bounded on the south by Bradley Lane, on the north by Thornapple Street and on the east by Brookeville Road, the earliest houses were built along Connecticut Avenue, Bradley Lane, **Raymond** and **Shepherd** streets.

Prior to World War I the area was not heavily settled, and there was so much open space that the Chevy Chase Hunt regularly rode through its fields. The 1920s were a boom period for Section 3, and 10 years later the section was almost completely built up. The Troths and the Simpsons built many of the early houses, while Monroe and Robert Bates Warren built bungalows and Period Revival houses on Shepherd, **Delaware** and **Florida** streets.

Boxwood has retained its architectural integrity.

Boxwood, also known as the Taylor-Britten house, is one of the largest and most impressive houses in Section 3. It sits on a two-acre lot on the north side of Bradley Lane near Connecticut Avenue. The lot was sold to Henry Clay Taylor in 1904, the year before Section 3 was officially opened. Taylor was a hero of the Spanish-American War who was promoted to Rear Admiral and appointed as Chief of the Navy's Bureau of Navigation. He died a short time afterwards, and his wife, Mary Virginia McGuire Taylor, built the house and lived there until her death in 1914. The second occupant was Alexander Britton, a distinguished attorney who was president of the Chevy Chase Club from 1918-1925. Samuel J. Henry, who authored a history of the Chevy Chase Hunt, was a later owner.

Horace Troth, Sr. worked for John Simpson as a carpenter, and eventually progressed to building houses himself. He worked on three houses on **Spring Street,** the last for his daughter Jeanette Troth Hill. She remembers that when she was a girl there were no paved streets near her house, only foot paths. Her father helped to make

Horace Edgar Troth built a Section 3 house for his family on Raymond Street in 1907.

walkways leading to Connecticut Avenue using ashes from their furnace. Jeanette's youngest brother, Lawrence Everett Troth, owned the Community Paint and Hardware Store on Connecticut Avenue in the District.

By 1911, the District of Columbia was enforcing tuition charges for Maryland pupils attending D.C. primary grades. In response, a small school opened on Delaware Street

The first Chevy Chase Elementary School at Rosemary Circle was in portables.

which attracted 108 students, but the building, Cromwell House, was not available the following year. Residents petitioned the County to support a new school, led by the newly-formed Home and School Association. The County contributed $20,000, and the residents of Chevy Chase raised an additional $5,000 to pay construction costs. Newlands again came to their aid, donating land on **Rosemary Street.** In 1913 four portable classrooms were erected on the south side of the street near the water tower. They accommodated grades one through seven, and two years later high school classes were added. The required furnishings were a pot-bellied stove to provide heat, and if neither gas nor electricity could be supplied, illumination came from kerosene lamps. Privies and a water source were outdoors. In 1917, as the population of Chevy Chase grew during World War I, Montgomery County finally realized a more substantial school was needed. It funded a completely new two-story building on **Valley Place,** a small street that ran from Rosemary Street north to **Meadow Lane.** The school was called Valley View, and it was planned to house the kindergarten through the sixth grade.

Elsie Irvine, a teacher, remembered: *There was something interesting about the old building, you know, the old red brick [2-story] building. There was a big center hall with a piano and the classes assembled for sing-alongs and plays, and the front steps of the building were an excellent place for class pictures during early spring and fall, a place for a good setting for a stage… And I always thought that Valley Place was the prettiest entrance. The Rosemary Street entrance was plainer on the front… There was, of course, a lot of land around it.*

The Winkler house was the home and business location for the Winkler family. It later became the site of Chevy Chase Elementary School. Photograph courtesy of Fred Winkler.

One of the few houses in the area was owned by Bernhard Winkler, a Swiss immigrant who had greenhouses and a plant nursery opposite the water tower. In 1909 he dismantled his house and one greenhouse and moved them by horse and wagon to the south side of Jones Bridge Road, where he eventually owned three acres abutting Rock Creek Park. Winkler's son Fred worked for his father all his life and became noted for the varieties of hybrid snapdragons that he developed. One of Winkler's neighbors was Dr. William Blum, a chemist at the National Bureau of Standards, who developed an electroplating process to make zinc-coated pennies and cartridge cases. It won him a medal at the end of his career.

The elementary school was located in **Section 4** which had been opened for development in 1909. The section was on the west side of Connecticut Avenue, north of Bradley Lane and extending north almost to what is now **East West Highway.** This was a much larger area than Section 3, and the landscape – characterized by meadows, gentle hills, woodland and small streams – justified naming its main street **Meadow Lane**. There were sufficient underground springs to supply the water tower on Rosemary Circle. The minimum cost of a house was set at $3,000 (as in Section 3), and the first houses were clustered in the area around the water tower. The land along Wisconsin Avenue was still held by the Walsh and Barrett families, but the Land Company finally acquired it in the 1920s.

Bernhard Winkler and his daughter Barbara inspecting the chrysanthemums in a greenhouse on Jones Mill Road at the new location in 1917. Photograph courtesy of Fred Winkler.

Shortly after Section 4 was platted, a new country club broke ground across the street from its northern border. In 1898 nine residents of the city had met to propose a club "for educational, literary and scientific purposes." It was called Columbia Golf Club, and the initiation fee was set at $2.00. The club originally was located along what is now **Georgia Avenue**, first on the east side and later on the west side, where the first golf course was laid out. Surrounded by farmland, the primitive nine-hole course protected its greens with a rope barrier to fend off the cows. After another move north, nearer the Soldiers' Home, a full eighteen-hole course was laid out on land rented for $50 a month. A bridge was built across **Illinois Avenue,** which was then more of a ditch than a road, with its unpaved surface at the bottom which served nicely as a hazard for the golf course. An old residence was used for the clubhouse, and the course was designed so that after playing three holes, the golfer arrived back at the house for a reviving drink at each turn.

Columbia's golf course was under construction by horse-drawn plows in 1910. Courtesy of Columbia Country Club.

In 1909 the members were warned that the property was slated for real estate development. When it became known the club was looking for a new location, the Land Company's offer of 126 acres of the former Hayes estate at a reasonable price was by far the most appealing. Realizing that population growth was moving to the northwest, and that the trolley line would run by the club's gates, Columbia Golf Club moved to its present location.

In August 1909, the certificate of incorporation was signed for the newly-named Columbia Country Club. About 200 members, three of them women, paid $100 each to join the new organization. Its total cash balance was about $1,200. From this modest beginning grew one of the finest country clubs in the nation. The leader of the effort to found the new club was Henry Litchfield West, for many years the Sports Editor of the *Washington Post*.

The clubhouse was placed on a knoll facing Connecticut Avenue and overlooking the golf course to the north. The course was designed by Walter J. Travis, one of the most

❖

renowned golfers in the country. In 1921 the National Open Tournament was played there, and the club has since hosted many other local and national tournaments. Other sports were not neglected. The tennis program has produced several national champions, and swimming and diving meets are a popular feature, as are bowling and platform tennis.

The Columbia Country Club engaged the talents of member Frederick B. Pyle to design the Spanish Colonial Revival clubhouse.

At the southern edge of Section 4, Henry Haywood Glassie lived near the Devereux family on Bradley Lane. When Glassie was General Counsel of the Post Office, he wrote the law establishing the Parcel Post. His son Henry was also a lawyer and in addition was a gifted amateur historian who ran a successful antiques business and was an authority on Washington architecture. Like many of their neighbors, the Glassies kept chickens. The Devereux family kept a cow. Young Don Glassie, Henry's brother, would ride to the neighbor's house on a pony to exchange a chicken for a gallon of milk.

The Glassie house was designed by George Oakley Totten, Jr.

The Devereux house was designed for the Devereuxs' ten children and still stands in spacious grounds on Bradley Lane.

The Devereux house, built in 1910, was the most imposing on Bradley Lane. It was on the site of a much smaller house that had been one of the earliest on the lane. Dr. John Ryan Devereux was the family doctor for many of the residents of Chevy Chase and was active in community affairs. With his 10 children in mind, in 1912 Dr. Devereux helped establish the Home and School Association, the first parent-teacher association in the county. The Association successfully petitioned Montgomery County to build the first local school, Valley View.

Dr. Devereux was appointed the first Health Officer for Section 4, whose duties included supervising quarantines. During World War I, Dr. John Devereux organized a Red Cross ambulance corps which he took to France. His son Joseph took charge of the corps and saw action on the front lines. Another son, Brigadier General James Devereux, commanded the Marines on Wake Island during World War II. The island fell to the Japanese and he was held prisoner for four years. General Devereux was awarded the Navy Cross, among many other decorations, and received a Presidential Unit Citation. After his retirement from the Marine Corps, General Devereux represented a Maryland District in the U. S. House of Representatives from 1951 to 1959.

Reginald Geare is thought to have been the architect for these houses on Leland Street, complete with sleeping porches.

At the same time in 1910, Fannie Barrett, a wealthy widow credited with being the person who began development adjacent to Section 4, purchased 120 acres west of the Land Company's property for a development of her own. She named her new development **Chevy Chase Park.**

Her early houses were simple two-story frame residences, but in a second wave of building in 1917, six Renaissance Revival houses were built on Leland Street, the only paved street in the interior of the section in 1915. In 1924 a new charter for Section 4 included Chevy Chase Park within its boundaries.

The end of World War I ushered in a building boom that lasted until 1941. As the Federal Government expanded, thousands of government workers stayed on in Washington and were looking for housing. Eighty-five percent of the houses in today's Section 4 were built during this period. Architect-designed homes were constructed in multiples in a broad range of styles. Developers such as Shannon and Luchs, Monroe and Bates Warren, George F. Mikkelson and Sons, and Frank Simpson Building Corporation were joined by many smaller companies. Individuals continued to purchase unimproved lots directly from the Land Company, and Chevy Chase continued to advertise itself as "a suburb of refinement and beauty."

In 1920 the Monroe and R. B. (Bates) Warren Company bought 67 acres west of Section 4. The land had been part of the Norwood Heights subdivision. On this property the Warren brothers developed **Leland**, a new subdivision. It was a full-scale undertaking for which sewers, water, paved streets, landscaping and utilities were provided. Leland was designed to attract automobile owners and was advertised as being only a 20-minute drive from the center of Washington. The most popular houses were inexpensive two-story models with a garage. A tradesman's entrance was provided so that ice could be delivered to the pantry when the residents were not at home. Dorothy Warren personally supervised the installation of domestic conveniences such as a dedicated radio outlet in the living room and solid brass hardware and fixtures.

Sally Dessez Miller described the ice delivery system in an oral history: *Everybody had a card, and we used to put it up in one of those windows. It had numbers all around it on the sides, ten, fifteen, twenty, and you'd turn it up so the number of pounds that you wanted was on the top, so they could see it. And the ice man would come up the street with a horse-drawn cart and would look at the sign. Then he would chip the ice off. We'd always go out there, because in the summer it was wonderful. We would get all the chips that came with the ice. Our ice box was in the corner of the pantry there, and they would just come in and stick it in.*

Adjacent to their new development called **Section 8**, the Warrens built a shopping strip along Wisconsin Avenue. It was called the **Tudor** because of the architecture of 12 one-story shops with half-timbered facades and gables and was home to a variety of small service-oriented businesses.

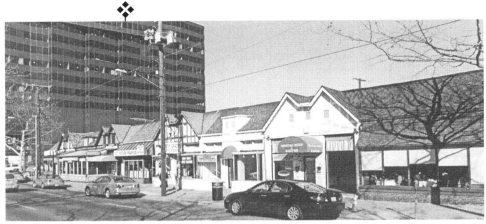

The Tudor shopping strip on Wisconsin Avenue is still a sought-after row of commercial spaces for small businesses like a cafe, a dry-cleaner and a paint supplier.

The dedication of a much wider sidewalk in front of the stores set the pattern for commercial frontage on Wisconsin Avenue. A 10-acre piece of land between **Walsh** and **Stanford** streets contained the large home of Dr. Ralph Walsh. He was a major investor in local real estate and the Georgetown trolley line. Walsh Street, in today's Town of Chevy Chase, is named for him.

Two of the Luzapone homes on Connecticut Avenue.

Two men who purchased their lots directly from the Land Company were Stephano Luzapone and Mihran Mesrobian. Their homes were outstanding additions to Connecticut Avenue. In 1925 Stephano built three Italian Renaissance Revival houses in a colorful row (which originally were orange, yellow and pink), so that he and his brothers, Constantino and Frank, could raise their children together. The brothers were skilled plaster craftsmen whose work decorates the U.S. Capitol, Union Station and many other public buildings. Fifteen years later Mesrobian, a DC architect, chose the *Art Moderne* style for his residence, a departure from his early *Beaux-Arts* training.

Monroe Warren was the founder and senior partner of his family construction business. He pioneered the construction of cooperative apartments in Washington, including the Kennedy-Warren in partnership with Edgar S. Kennedy. The partnership failed during the Depression and forced Warren to declare bankruptcy. Undeterred, he wasted little time in starting another company, Meadowbrook Construction Inc., which operated from 1932 to 1966. Then he built the **Meadowbrook** community. Architects Harvey P. Baxter and Harry Edwards planned approximately 60 solidly-built Colonial Revival brick, stone and clapboard houses in Meadowbrook. The neighborhood was bounded by East West Highway, **Aspen Street,** Meadow Lane and **Maple Street**.

There were so many underground streams in the center of Section 4 that it remained undeveloped for many years. Finally in 1928, builder George Mikkelson bought the open space between Meadow Lane and **Ridgewood Avenue** from the Land Company. Mikkelson's houses were carefully designed to conform to the natural landscape, and featured shared driveways and detached garages. When the house was on a slope overlooking a stream, a connecting bridge would give access to the property. Ralph W. Berry and A. W. Smith were Mikkelson's principal architects. Their Colonial and Tudor Revival homes were aimed at an upper-middle-class market. In 1929 and 1930, Shannon and Luchs further subdivided

Heaton's signature design, with enclosed central entry vestibule, can still be seen on Leland Street.

part of Chevy Chase Park and Section 4. Architect Arthur Heaton was engaged to design some simple three-bay Colonial Revival houses.

By 1930, to accommodate an ever-increasing student enrollment, architect Howard Wright Cutler designed a new Chevy Chase Elementary School. Valley View School was demolished, and most of Valley Place disappeared under the playgrounds of the new school. It was a U-shaped brick building with Art Deco elements and classically embellished entrances. In the coming decades, several additions and changes in the design were necessary. Classrooms were added and multi-purpose rooms reconfigured. The Chevy Chase Elementary School Educational Foundation helped raise the money for an extensive renovation.

In 1980 declining enrollment prompted the closing of many Southern County elementary schools. Others were paired, and the resulting policy ensured neighborhood schools for Chevy Chase. North Chevy Chase Elementary School, after opening in the early 1960's on Jones Bridge Road, either needed renovation or faced closure and merger with another school. The community preferred renovation and joined Chevy Chase Elementary in with Rosemary Hills Elementary School. Now Rosemary Hills hosts the Chevy Chase students of both schools for kindergarten through second grade, and the Chevy Chase schools host the Rosemary Hills students for third through sixth grade.

The 1999 renovation of Chevy Chase Elementary School restored its distinctive architectural decorative features.

The Land Company gave the library wing of the current Chevy Chase Elementary School. A tablet presented at the rededication on April 29, 2001 states: "In honor of Senator Francis Griffith Newlands and his descendants, founder and developer of the Chevy Chase Community and, from the beginning, loyal supporter of its libraries."

The need for a high school separate from the elementary school at Valley Place was apparent within a few years. The first high school opened on **Wilson Lane** in 1926 in what was then a rural area of **Bethesda**. Two years later it was moved to a new building on **44th Street.** The original building fronted on 44th Street, with wings for classrooms extending along 44th to **Willow Lane** and **Elm Street.** Behind the central block were a gymnasium and an auditorium. About the time East West Highway was completed in 1936, linking Bethesda to **Silver Spring,** Bethesda-Chevy Chase High School (B-CC) opened on the old **Watkins Farm** property. The campus, facing East West Highway, reflected the pressure of increasing population and eventually contained several buildings.

Bethesda-Chevy Chase High School, with an extensive renovation, is ready to serve another century of students, but in 1951 it looked like this.

The school on 44th street became Leland Junior High, for grades 7, 8 and 9. Over-crowding during World War II led to the construction of a new junior high fronting on **Elm Street** in 1963, and the old school complex was demolished. The ninth grade was moved to B-CC in 1979. Declining enrollment in the 1970s led to Leland's closure in 1981. The school merged with Western Junior High on **Massachusetts Avenue** and was renamed Westland Middle School. The Chevy Chase schools were growing into part of the wider county school system.

Leland Junior High moved to a new building in 1963 and remained there until 1981. Courtesy of the Town of Chevy Chase.

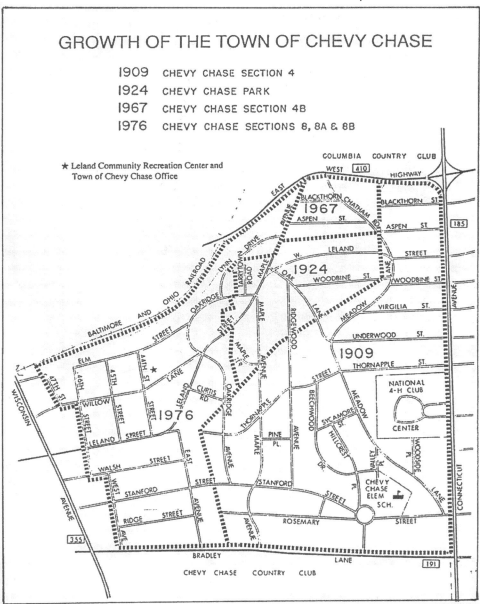

GROWTH OF THE TOWN OF CHEVY CHASE

1909   CHEVY CHASE SECTION 4

1924   CHEVY CHASE PARK

1967   CHEVY CHASE SECTION 4B

1976   CHEVY CHASE SECTIONS 8, 8A & 8B

★ Leland Community Recreation Center and
  Town of Chevy Chase Office

The growth of Section 4 depended on developers and a number of independent builders. Courtesy of the Town of Chevy Chase.

The Hartwell-Laird house, the first to be built on Meadow Lane, dates to 1912.

CHAPTER 7

FINAL PIECES

The Hamlet introduced a new architectural concept.

❖

Francis Newlands died during his third term as U.S. senator from Nevada. The Land Company reorganized itself after his death in 1917 and finally platted Section 5 in 1923. The Land Company's part of Section 5 was only one block deep and only 4 blocks long, running from Connecticut Avenue on the west to the center of **Dalkeith Street** on the east, and from **Thornapple Street** to **Woodbine Street.** It abutted both Otterbourne and the Williams tract on the east, which were absorbed into the new section. The result was a mix of 19th-century Victorian frame houses and farmhouses with modern period revival brick homes.

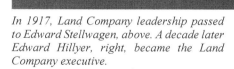

In 1917, Land Company leadership passed to Edward Stellwagen, above. A decade later Edward Hillyer, right, became the Land Company executive.

During World War I, before Section 5 officially opened, the Land Company loaned a strip of land to the Navy League's National Service School, a training camp for young women. Incorporated in 1917, its honorary commandants were Mrs. George Dewey, widow of the famous admiral, and Mrs. Hugh Scott, wife of the Chief of Staff of the United States

❖

Army. The camp was located on **Underwood Street** on both sides of Connecticut Avenue, with tents on one side for sleeping and on the other for classes and meals. The camp's purpose was to instruct young women over 18 years of age in skills that would contribute to the war effort. Courses of instruction included surgical dressings, first aid, telegraphy, knitting, hygiene and dietetics. Military calisthenics and drill were also included. President Wilson welcomed the first enrollees in 1917. The program continued for two years, and over 2,000 women attended the camp.

The National Service School was designed to train women in support services for the troops. Courtesy of Julie Thomas.

Before the Land Company officially opened Section 5, its residents had organized themselves into a Citizens Association. They met informally at the E. M. Wells home on March 24, 1916. Families in the Association came from Otterbourne, Williams Lane and the property on the east side of Brookeville Road with houses on the remnants of the No Gain grant. Their first concern was to obtain street lights for the Percy Street trolley stop. Ten lights were furnished for the purpose by PEPCO for $150 per year. By 1922 PEPCO took over supplying electricity in all jurisdictions of Chevy Chase. The power plant at the Lake was closed, and PEPCO supplied the electricity for the trolley line.

❖

Transportation was another pressing concern. The condition of the tracks and the speed of the automobile caused some serious accidents. An early history of Section 5 reported that *streets and sidewalks were not paved. Road conditions were often so poor that cars would drive on the sidewalks to avoid getting stuck in the mud. Because funds were so short, members of the Association were often called on to voluntarily get together and repair the roadways. Residents graded bad spots and spread cinders in an effort to improve the poor roads.*

Improving roads and avenues was an ongoing civic concern, the need evident from this view of Williams Lane looking east toward Brookeville Road in 1920.

From its inception Section 5's Citizens Association had been considering the question of becoming a special taxing district like Sections 2 and 3. Residents petitioned Section 3 to have Otterbourne and the Williams Lane tract added to that district. When Section 3 rejected the offer, the residents of Section 5 decided to take steps to form a special taxing district of their own. In 1922, the new Special Taxing District of Section 5 met to elect its officers, and a short time

❖

later the Land Company added its property to the area. **North Chevy Chase** and **Chevy Chase View** were recognized in 1924 as special taxing districts, but they were not part of the Land Company holdings or oversight.

The map for Section 5 indicates its various origins.

Taxing authority was granted to the various sections, although their incorporation was formalized much later. Section 3 received taxing authority in 1914 and its incorporation in 1981. Martin's Additions received taxing authority in 1916 and incorporation in 1985. Section 4 received taxing authority as an incorporated municipality in 1918. After a series of annexations, which doubled its size, Section 4 voted to be renamed the **Town of Chevy Chase** in 1983. Section 5 received municipality taxing authority in 1922 and incorporated in 1982.

With the legal recognition of the sections, the various citizens associations developed into village councils, boards of managers and other similar, but differently named, governing bodies. In all cases, they are elected but unsalaried. As the need for services grew beyond the capability or time of the volunteer leaders, professional staff was hired to provide the actual services or to utilize county agencies. Town councils report to regularly scheduled meetings, hold hearings about community issues and celebrate successful conclusions to disputes. The codes and permits make clear that Chevy Chase sections are responsibly governed as well as friendly places to live. Chevy Chase has always been attractive to foreign diplomats, and neighbors have enjoyed friendships with renters from a broad spectrum of countries. The only official residences have been those of Jordan and Nigeria, both now elsewhere.

Minnie Brooke was an active national supporter of women's suffrage. Courtesy of Robert A. Truax, from the Library of Congress.

Although the No Gain grant had been divided into many smaller pieces in Chevy Chase, the original farmhouse and some acreage surrounding it still remained. After passing out of the Griffith family, No Gain was owned by Wentworth Brooke and his wife Minnehaha, who was known as Minnie. The Brookes called the property **Brooke Farm** and operated the house as an inn for a time. Minnie opened the Brooke Farm Tea House in a cottage-like building on the south end of the farm. Minnie was an experienced and successful restaurateur, and had operated numerous teahouses before opening the one in Chevy Chase.

The teahouse structure has survived as a popular restaurant, La Ferme, with a French menu.

By the late 1920s the Brookes had sold the farm to Dr. and Mrs. Frank Schultz, who remodeled the old plantation house. Schultz sold flowers to florists in the city and grew grapes for his own wine when prohibition outlawed the sale of alcohol. In 1928, aware of the crowding at Chevy Chase Elementary School, he opened the Bradford Home School in the building that had housed the tea house. The school gradually expanded to include 74 pupils. The grounds of the farm provided an idyllic playground for the students, riding "Dixie" the pony and feeding the farm animals. The school was forced to close when the new building for Chevy Chase Elementary opened in 1932. Mrs. Schultz took over the Bradford building and opened a new tea house which became the place of choice for many luncheons given by the area's residents. The property is now once again known as No Gain.

In 1928, **Section 5A** was platted by the Land Company. It filled in the piece of land remaining between Connecticut Avenue and Brookeville Road that lay north of Leland Street, and crossed East West Highway (then called the **Bethesda-Silver Spring Highway**) to **Dunlop Street,** the street that was named for the family that owned Hayes. The new subdivision was created by engineers David J. Howell and Sons. It featured winding streets and irregularly shaped lots.

One small area of 5A had a unique plan called **The Hamlet** which would lend its name to other parts of Chevy Chase. Conceived by Newlands' daughter, Janet Newlands Johnston**,** it is bordered by Connecticut Avenue**, Glendale Road**, East West Highway and **Blackthorn Street.** California/Nevada architect Dan Kirkuff designed a group of houses in 1933 inspired by the architecture at the College of William and Mary. Each house faced a common central court paved for parking automobiles and had part of its garden bordered by a hedge or wall. Janet's sister, Edith, oversaw the details of construction and installation which included electric ranges, refrigerators, and air conditioning. Like some other parts of 5A, restrictive covenants could be found in the deeds to The Hamlet, which prohibited sale to African Americans or Jews. The covenants became obsolete after a Supreme Court decision in 1948 ruled them unenforceable.

The last parcel of land to be developed in Section 5 was **Smoot's Addition to Chevy Chase,** which was laid out in 1962. It lies to the east of Brookeville Road, at the northernmost boundary of the section. Listed as "Lot number 7, block A," owned by George A. Smoot, it is a small neat development of eight traditional houses designed by architect Harvey P. Baxter. A new street, **Windsor Place,** was cut to access the area, curving down a hill to a small stream and park-like area at the bottom. One owner purchased the stream bed in order to protect it from development.

A DEVELOPMENT OF THE CHEVY CHASE LAND COMPANY

at Connecticut Avenue & East-West Highway, Chevy Chase, Maryland

THOS. J. FISHER & CO. INC., AGENT - 738 15 STREET, WASHINGTON, D. C.

The Land Company advertised for renters with this aerial view of The Hamlet. Courtesy of Chevy Chase Land Company.

Simultaneously with the development of Section 5, the Land Company made plans to fill the still undeveloped land west of Chevy Chase Village. **Section 1**, which had been used by the Kirkside Golf Club, was platted for subdivision in October of 1925, probably with the knowledge that the golf club was intending to close in 1926. **Section 1A**, which extended west to Wisconsin Avenue, quickly followed. Because of its frontage on Wisconsin Avenue, it lent itself to commercial development. As a result, the office building known as **Chevy Chase Center** came into being. The cluster of shops included a drugstore, a Giant grocery, a dress shop and a shop selling household linens.

Saks Fifth Avenue, the only large store on the property, is contiguous to the residential part of Section 1 and was incorporated into the Village along with the small street called **South Park Avenue**. The architecture of the houses

❖

The high rise in the Land Company's complex includes offices and a restaurant, while the companion building at the corner has a bus terminal and (long after this 1960 photo) a Metro stop.

is mixed: period revival, ranch and contemporary. Mikkelson built six houses in the Williamsburg tradition on Oliver Street in 1937.

The Chevy Chase Ward of the Church of Jesus Christ of the Latter-day Saints was formed in 1940, when it was apparent that the large chapel on 16th Street was inadequate for its expanding congregation. Members of the Ward met at the Chevy Chase Woman's Club for some years while plans were being made for their chapel. In August of 1951 the first meeting was held in the Chevy Chase Ward Chapel of the Church of Jesus Christ of the Latter-day Saints. Located on **Western Avenue** at the corner of **Kirkside Drive**, the church building could not be dedicated until it was completely free of debt. This was quickly accomplished, and an "Over the Top" dinner was celebrated in December of the same year.

The chapel of the Chevy Chase Ward of the Church of Jesus Christ of the Latter-day Saints on Western Avenue is a recent addition to the religious structures in Chevy Chase.

❖

The Baptists, who had sold their chapel on Connecticut Avenue at Shepherd Street to the Methodists many years before, founded a new Chevy Chase Baptist Church in 1923. At first services were held in the Avalon Theater, but within 12 months a new chapel was built on Western Avenue on the south or District side like the Presbyterians. The congregation grew rapidly, and a new sanctuary was built in 1948 at the same location, with an education wing added in 1959. After a slow period which resulted in the closing of the building in 1996, the church reopened a year later. New leadership and new priorities have invigorated the church, and it now celebrates "Faith Fulfilled."

For children, Chevy Chase was an unfenced playground. As George Stone remembered his childhood in Martin's Additions: *We climbed trees, chewed sassafras leaves imagining them wads of tobacco, cut paths through briar patches making a maze with difficult passages, caught butterflies for a collection, skated, biked, played (on cool evenings) dodge ball, or red rover in each other's front yards, learned to dance, did the leg-work for the weekend ice-cream sales (McKeever's vanilla from Kensington was delicious and special), explored the surrounding woods, and jumped from shed-roof to roof-top up at George Medlar's playing cops and robbers.* In 1930 a drought caused Rock Creek to lose much of its water. The fish died and the swimming hole disappeared.

The old swimming hole in Rock Creek Park (at present Meadowbrook Center) was popular for fishing in the 1920s.

Children played unsupervised in vacant lots and open streams, with the parental admonition "come home when you hear the dinner bell." Boys built forts and clubhouses with materials "borrowed" from construction sites, or raced die-cast metal racing cars on elaborate tracks dug out of the muddy banks of the school playground. Don Chapman discovered his aptitude for engineering by damming Chevy Chase creeks and recalled: *Many hours were spent skipping stones at the 'water striders,' hopping across rocks, building small dams, or exploring the storm drainpipes that opened into the "creek." It was not unusual to find minnows and frogs in the lower reaches of Coquelin Run.* [Houses being built in the vacant lots were] *a temptation beyond denial. We explored every aspect of their construction until at last the exasperated workmen ran us out.*

Young men participated in sports leagues in the 1920s. The Chevy Chase Bearcats had a baseball record of 29 wins and 9 losses in 1925.

During the Depression boys sought jobs delivering newspapers. One group of enterprising teenagers published their own neighborhood weekly. Larry and Leonard Williams reported on life in Martin's Additions from 1931 to mid-1936, with their mother printing off the subscription copies on her mimeograph. The *Thornapple Street News* staff included Catherine Fowler and Dan Tucker, acting as reporters or editors as the need arose. The *Shepherd Street News* was a similar publication which ran from July 29, 1972 to January 5, 1974. The newspapers had a subscription rate and a large percentage of target subscribers.

The Williams family seldom missed a publishing deadline.

Another weekly newspaper, *The Leland Street Sunday News (LSSN),* began publishing in 1973 for the 4100 block of Leland Street. After thirty years, with families rotating as its reporters and editors, adults took over the publication in order to continue a treasured neighborhood asset. Typically, the decision to continue publication occurred at a block party ice cream social. With better duplication technology, the LSSN now often features photographs.

World War II brought an influx of government workers needing housing, and Chevy Chase residents rented rooms or whole houses "for the duration." It was an anxious time for the home front, anticipating and dreading news. A whistle from the postman signaled the occupant that he had a letter from overseas. The trolleys were gone, so residents commuted by bus, or shared automobile rides if a neighbor had a car and rationed gas. Parents and older children served as air raid wardens and knocked at night on doors where black-out curtains were inadequate. The families who lived along Williams Lane were particularly close and kept tabs

Jean Dinwoodey and Julia Ann Schaenzer presented First Lady Eleanor Roosevelt with a box of cookies for the 31st anniversary of the Girl Scouts in 1942.

The B-CC Rescue Squad, prepared for wartime service in 1942. Courtesy of Julie Thomas.

on the neighbors in the armed forces. With many families separated at Christmas time, one resident wrote in paraphrase "O Little town of Chevy Chase, How oft we think of thee..." for all to be singing, wherever they were, and remember each other on the holiday.

Children collected paper, tinfoil and other recyclables, and families dug up lawns for "victory gardens." In Chevy Chase garden produce was collected each fall weekend for a neighborhood canning operation. Organized by the elementary school cook, the school's kitchen became an assembly line where vegetables and fruits were cleaned, peeled and readied for sterile jars and processing. At the end of the day, participating families took home a load of preserved food to stretch their allowance for rationed items.

In response to the needs of war refugees, a temporary cooperative nursery school reopened at Chevy

Alison (Mac) McQueen was the whistling postman of Chevy Chase Village. Mac was honored by the cartoonist Clifford Berryman of the Washington Evening Star.

Ration books accompanied shoppers to the grocery store.

Chase Elementary for the war years, sharing the playground and other facilities so as not to disturb the regular school schedule.

When the war was over, service men and women returned to a Chevy Chase little changed. There were still open streams, vacant lots and untamed hillsides. Homes could no longer be shared with boarders or businesses, and residential guidelines reverted to their pre-war strictures. The tempo of development, curtailed or postponed by the war, accelerated. Changes and new growth would be particularly evident in the area north of East West Highway.

Brigadier General James Devereux was greeted by his friends and neighbors with a victory parade on his return from World War II. Courtesy of Julie Thomas.

CHAPTER 8

GROWTH AND CHANGE

*Chevy Chase Park was the Land
Company's last subdivision.*

By the early 1920s Francis Newlands' original plan for residential development was complete, but there remained much opportunity for growth in the area from East West

Construction on the pool began in 1927; now all that remains is a flat meadow.

Highway to Jones Bridge Road. A fire in 1925 and the closing of the trolley line in 1935 led to the end of dance music at Chevy Chase Lake in 1937. The dam for the lake collapsed, and Coquelin Run again became a quiet stream running toward Rock Creek. Into this vacated space a mixture of commercial and residential construction developed, with the addition of several new community institutions. To respond to the community's desire for a place to swim, a 100-by-200-foot pool was built between the Columbia Country Club golf links and the railroad tracks, on land along Connecticut Avenue leased from the Land Company. The Heon family opened the Chevy Chase Pool to the public in 1925. Later it was operated on a restricted membership fee basis, which led to its closure in 1972.

Senator Newlands had always wanted to provide convenient shopping for Chevy Chase. This concept expanded after World War II. More shops sprang up below Chevy Chase Circle, and opportunities opened up to the north on Connecticut Avenue with property freed up from the former trolley and amusement park operations. Only Thomas Perry's lumber yard remained to supply the construction needs of the developers and builders of Chevy Chase. Thomas Perry, Jr. worked there all his life. He bought the land from the Land Company, but the Company later repurchased the land for possible future use.

A small commercial development called Chevy Chase Lake East opened in 1951 just north of Perry's business. The anchor store opened in 1958. Founder Bernard Freedman was the first member of his family to own the Chevy Chase Lake Supermarket. It originally faced Connecticut Avenue, flanked by an optician and a hair salon. In 1963 Freedman and his new partner Walter Kirsch moved the store across the parking lot to its present location. They enlarged it in 1970, with the store never closing because remodeling was done at night. The market is now owned and operated by the Kirsch family. The Lake Pharmacy was opened by William Packett about the same time as the super market. Packett's was a model for service to the community and for many years had the added attraction of a luncheonette.

In 1971 the Chevy Chase Land Company built a 13-story office building on the footprint of the trolley car terminal. This explains why the building faces Connecticut at a slight angle. It houses the offices of the Land Company, a Chevy Chase Bank branch, and other businesses including a restaurant.

The car barn on the south side of the tracks was adapted for use by the T. W. Perry Company and the other one was torn down.

The B. F. Saul Building towers over its one-story neighbors.

❖

Chevy Chase Lake West was begun in 1952, with the bank building added in 1959. A drycleaners, a bank, a florist, and a hardware store (with a post office substation) all bordered Connecticut Avenue. Since then restaurants, a dress shop and other specialty stores have enjoyed the location, with parking in the rear. Gas stations on both sides of the street, two on the west and one on the east, vie for customers.

Behind Chevy Chase Lake West, a stretch of open land had been part of the Hayes grant. It passed into the Laird family through the marriage of Barbara Laird and James Dunlop. The Land Company officially opened the property to development in 1926, platted as **Section 4-A**. Some of the houses were built earlier. One, built on the foundations of the first after a 1910 fire, still stands on **Laird Place**. Section 4-A includes Hayes and the adjacent Columbia Country Club, but its heart is the neighborhood of **Chevy Chase Hills** with its own informal citizens network conducted by telephone rather than an elected management.

A volunteer fire department served Chevy Chase since the first hydrants were installed, but the hose wagons had to be hand propelled. By 1926 an effort was made to form a more formal fire department. Chevy Chase and Martin's Additions joined together to form the "Association for Fire Protection for the District of Chevy Chase." Six former D. C. firefighters were hired, and two dozen volunteers were recruited. New equipment was acquired but was still stored in

Firehouse personnel were on call for both fire and medical emergencies in this photo taken in 1959.

the Village Hall or on the street in Martin's Additions. In 1931 the need was recognized for more substantial quarters. The fire department authorized the construction of a

❖

SAFETY-FIRST LOCAL DIRECTORY

Clip this card to front cover of your Telephone Directory for quick reference.

IN CASE OF FIRE

Main 20   D. C. Fire Department.

Cleve 917   Chevy Chase Fire Department (Sec. 2).

Know the location of your nearest **Fire Plug**. Fire plugs are located as follows: Conn. Ave. and Shepherd St.; Conn. Ave. and Bradley Lane; Bradley Lane and Brookville Road; Bradley Lane opposite W. H. Booth; Section 4 near Raymond St. and Conn. Ave.

FOR GENERAL ALARM—Continued but **broken** ringing of church bell. Emergency **Keys to Church** can be had at homes of **J. L. Beatie** and **W. D. Nichols**. In response, those having fire extinguishers should take them along. Stars in the list below indicate possession of fire exting-ishers. Is yours conveniently placed and **ready for use?**

COMMUNITY LADDER at home of D. J. Courtney, Delaware St.

TELEPHONE LIST

Cleveland 560   Health Office.

917   Night Watchman, Section 2.

321   Fire Marshall, Sec. 3, T. W. Perry.

946	Beatie, J. L.*	6320 Delaware St.
507	Bielaski, A. B.*	12 Raymond St.
610	Booth, H. W.*	25 Bradley Lane
616	Burkart, J. A.*	6311 Conn. Ave.
	Cadel, F.	107 Shepherd St.
152	Carter, W. G.*	16 Taylor St.
991	Cassels, D. J.*	21 Bradley Lane
1149-W	Clark, W. M.*	209 Shepherd St.
	Conard, P. J.*	206 Raymond St.
513	Courtney, D. J.	6309 Delaware St
391-J	Crandall, B.*	215 Raymond St.
830	Cromwell, J. C.*	6312 Delaware St.
1225--W	Curtis, H. L.*	6316 Delaware St.
174-W	Cusack, N. S.	110 Raymond St.
	Eiker, J. M.*	6312 Conn. Ave.
1009	Etchison, H.	6308 Brookville Rd.
488	Fortune, L.*	206 Shepherd St.
	Gibbs, H. C.	211 Raymond St.
1255	Graham, H. A.	204 Shepherd St.
558	Grovermann, W. H.*	6305 Conn. Ave.
586	Henkel, E.*	6309 Conn. Ave.
1041-W	Herschel, W. H.*	6305 Florida St.
1225-J	Hopper, M. B.	6313 Conn. Ave.
431-J	Imlay M. W.*	106 Raymond St.
556	Keliher, J. A.*	Brookville Rd.
617	Leavell, B. A.	39 Bradley Lane
298	Leet, A. B.*	105 Raymond St.
138	Leet, M.*	100 Raymond St.
	Leonard, E. J.	200 Raymond St.
196	Lord, H. M.	109 Shepherd St.
568-J	Ludlum, S. S.	6314 Conn. Ave.
	Mastin, G. M.	15 Taylor St.
1275	Meatyard, F. A.	6315 Conn. Ave.
1136	Meeds, H. S.	6 Shepherd St.
1253	Meloy, F. E.	204 Raymond St.
	Merritt, E.*	208 Shepherd St.
	Mikkelson, G. F.*	104 Raymond St.
1094	Mills, W. A.	29 Bradley Lane
43	Murphy, E. J.*	6205 Conn. Ave.
303-W	Nichols, W. D.*	6402 Conn. Ave.
731	Norcross, T. W.	101 Taylor St.
431-W	Paine, H. S.*	102 Raymond St.
321	Perry, T. W.*	11 Shepherd St.
	Scammell, R. S.	6 Raymond St.
391-W	Shull, J. M.*	207 Raymond St.
968	Troth, H. E.	205 Raymond St.
1155-W	Troth, J. E.	6306 Brookville Rd.
548	Wallace, E.*	6314 Deleware St.

With this 1920s poster, the Section 3 community hoped to be prepared for disasters.

❖

firehouse on Connecticut Avenue at Dunlop Street designed by Ralph W. Berry and built by Alfred T. Newbold. It provided for garaging five fire engines and living space for the firemen. In 1954 the force dropped volunteers and became a professional organization. In 1981 the Chevy Chase Fire Department was designated as the Hazardous Materials (HAZ MAT) center for all of Montgomery County, and a separate bay was built for the HAZ MAT engine.

The Woman's Club has a varied program emphasizing education and the arts.

Just south of the firehouse, a large Colonial Revival building was being constructed in 1937, the headquarters of the Woman's Club of Chevy Chase. In 1913 three young homemakers were inspired to create a club for community improvement and sociability. Initially they had met in one another's homes, with the dues fixed at 25 cents a month. From a charter membership of 12, the club quickly grew to its limit of 800 members, and in 1916 it was admitted to the General Federation of Women's Clubs. Still without a building of its own, the club held business meetings in local churches. Today, housed in its handsome headquarters complete with a stage for dramatics and public speaking, the club features programs on educational and cultural subjects, and each year a popular art show and an antiques show provide revenue for its welfare projects. The Club's community outreach centers on education, and it has won a Citation of Merit from Montgomery County for its tutoring program at Chevy Chase Elementary School.

❖

The First Church of Christ, Scientist was organized in May 1940 as a branch of the Mother Church in Boston, Massachusetts. All Christian Scientist churches are autonomous but must be recognized by the Mother Church. A group of worshippers who were members of churches in Washington led the organizational effort in Chevy Chase. Services were held in the Village Hall, by then the traditional place for blossoming congregations to meet. Land was bought on the north corner of **Club Drive** and Connecticut Avenue. As soon as wartime restrictions on building were lifted, work was begun on the Colonial Revival building. In 1949 the cornerstone was laid and the church, debt free, was dedicated the following March. The auditorium of the church seats 400, and the spacious interior includes room for the Sunday school, a library, and meeting rooms. The Christian Science Reading room, now located in Bethesda, is open to the public.

The First Church of Christ, Scientist, on the 7900 block of Connecticut Avenue, balances the block with the Woman's Club of Chevy Chase in architectural style and simplicity.

It was not until 1965 that the Chevy Chase library was established, a branch of the Montgomery County public library system. Before then readers were dependent on the D. C. public library just below Chevy Chase Circle and the large regional county library in Bethesda. In 1990 the library on Connecticut Avenue was closed for renovations, and due to county budget problems did not reopen until March of 1992. The services for all ages of patrons, from young families to seniors, were sorely missed during the closure.

❖

The headquarters of the Chevy Chase Historical Society, founded in 1981, is located on the lower level of the library. Its Archive and Research Center collects, records and shares materials relating to the history of Chevy Chase, Maryland. The non-circulating collection includes photographs, maps, oral histories, newsletters, architectural drawings and books. The Society sponsors a variety of programs and activities to foster knowledge and appreciation of the community's history.

The Chevy Chase Library is host to many civic groups.

The Land Company filed a request in 1932 for apartment construction zoning, but the permission was not acted upon until after World War II. In 1950 the Land Company built a group of apartments on **Chevy Chase Lake Drive** called Chevy Chase Lake Apartments. The Land Company sold them to builder Monroe Warren. He in turn resold them to the Montgomery County Housing Opportunity Commission for middle-income rental housing. Next to this complex is a single unit named Hamlet House. On **Manor Road** another series of apartments was constructed the same year called the Chevy Chase Lake North Apartments.

❖

Further along Manor Road the Land Company constructed 67 town houses on **Preston Place.** In the 1960s the Land Company offered the remaining land on the east end of Chevy Chase Lake Drive, and Monroe Warren built townhouses on the property. They were originally designed as rental units, but later became a cooperative known as **Hamlet Place.** Off Manor Road is **Gavin Manor Court,** named for Gavin Farr, chairman of the Land Company.

The **Dunlop Farm,** north of East West Highway, was opened for development by the Land Company in the 1940s. **Glendale Road** and **Curtis Street** were extended across the highway, and many of the builders from the older section continued to work in the new one. "The new Hamlet," as it came to be called, was bounded by Connecticut Avenue on the west, Chevy Chase Lake Drive on the north and **Farmington** on the east. The landscape is characterized by rolling hills and curving streets that recall its rural origins.

This aerial view shows various types of apartments in the Chevy Chase Lake area along Connecticut Avenue north of East West Highway.

The northern limits of Section 5 extend only to Leland Street, so the neighborhoods to the north were never incorporated. They lacked a community association which the other neighborhoods had been granted by law. In 1953 some of the homeowners met to discuss the unwelcome possibility that a major highway would run nearby. An informal citizens association evolved from this meeting, which became The Hamlet Citizens Association of Chevy Chase, Maryland. The Association meets annually and has connections with several local organizations such as the Fire Board and the Chevy Chase Library.

Connecticut Avenue is better for pedestrians than cars after an unusual snowfall in 1966.

By 2000 the Land Company had sold its last undeveloped property. A brick-wall-enclosed group of single family homes was built and named **Chevy Chase Park,** repeating a name used many years before in Section 4. It lies between Manor Road and Jones Bridge Road. The site was earlier sought for a Bloomingdale's Department Store and then for the headquarters of the Pan American Health Organization, but resident opposition prevailed.

Two large apartment complexes face each other on Connecticut Avenue. In 1987 the Hyatt Company built a Classic Residence on the west side of the street. It is a luxurious senior living community which overlooks the grounds of the Columbia Country Club. Directly opposite is the Land Company-built 8101 Connecticut Avenue condominiums. It is located on part of the site of the old Chevy Chase Lake amusement park and borders Coquelin Run. The two buildings offer another residential option for residents of Chevy Chase and appeal particularly to older residents who no longer want to care for a large house.

The last new neighbor to arrive in the Lake area was the Howard Hughes Medical Institute. Named for and funded by the estate of the billionaire businessman, pilot and movie producer, the Institute funds medical research in facilities worldwide. This branch began construction in 1991. It is situated on 22.5 acres of land on the south side of Jones Bridge Road, and houses laboratories, a library, an auditorium, dining rooms and overnight accommodations for conferees. The Institute has recently purchased the historic Hayes Manor house and its remaining property. After initial concern by residents, the quiet presence of the Institute and its attractive

The Howard Hughes Medical Institute is hidden in an urban forest.

architecture and landscaping have made it a welcome and almost invisible addition to Chevy Chase.

The entire mix of houses, apartments, shops and institutions, fitted into the space from Jones Bridge Road on the north, Jones Mill Road on the east, East West Highway to the south and the Columbia Country Club on the west, is called collectively Chevy Chase Lake. The residents are content to enjoy their various neighborhoods without a formal governing body, while identifying themselves to the world as inheritors of the Chevy Chase name and lifestyle. The lake is long gone, and the pool that succeeded it. But the name identifies a very lively segment of Chevy Chase that is often overlooked as automobiles speed north or south on the main street of Chevy Chase, Connecticut Avenue.

While just beyond the Land Company boundary of Jones Bridge Road, the estate In the Woods had a strong influence on Chevy Chase. David Fairchild and his wife, Marion Bell Fairchild, built an unusual house in 1910 with a one-room

❖❖

workshop on the grounds for her father, Alexander Graham Bell. The Fairchilds cultivated many exotic plant imports (unfortunately including the infamous kudzu). Dr. Fairchild established the USDA Office of Plant Introduction, introduced 75,000 species of plants and was instrumental in arranging for the gift of Japanese cherry trees to ring the **Tidal Basin.** Today four of the In the Woods' 34 acres belong to the

The Fairchilds built their distinctive house in 1910 on Spring Valley Road, surrounded by acres of imported, often exotic, plants and trees.

Chevy Chase Recreation Association (CCRA), which is linked for membership to various jurisdictions of Chevy Chase. It has been a club for swimming and tennis since 1959. The grounds continue to be an arboretum of rare trees and shrubs, and the Outdoor Nursery School utilizes the house.

Like Chevy Chase Village, the Town of Chevy Chase expanded beyond its original boundaries. In 1924 it had added Barrett's Chevy Chase Park, and in 1967 additional blocks extended the town boundary north to East West Highway. In 1976 the three parts of **Section 8** petitioned the Town for annexation when it was threatened with high-rise construction along Wisconsin Avenue. The Town established its jurisdiction and defined its boundaries by adding 326 houses and 1,000 residents through annexation, almost doubling the town's size.

The Tudor Revival strip of shops built along Wisconsin Avenue at Leland Street sparked further commercial development, and several multi-storied buildings. The Writer's Center, founded in 1977, moved to Walsh Avenue in 1993, adapting a former Montgomery County recreation center. It

❖❖

❖

offers classes and workshops in a wide spectrum of literary disciplines, from poetry to memoir, and for all ages. In a recent remodeling, it added a workable stage for theatrical presentations. The Center's neighbors are an assortment of small businesses, restaurants and food purveyors along with the telephone exchange, a handsome stone building erected in 1928, and the Keshishian building. There was a rusty storage warehouse northeast of the Writer's Center, owned at one time by Smith Moving and Storage, but its ghost is now overgrown with houses.

When Leland Junior High on Elm Street merged with a middle school outside the Town, and it was determined that the school building was not a candidate for an alternative use, the building was torn down. In partnership with the county and Maryland-National Capital Park and Planning Commission, the Town of Chevy Chase built the Leland Community Center in 1989, renamed the Jane E. Lawton Community Recreation Center in 2009, to house the Town

Jane Lawton, a civic leader in the county and state, was the Town Chair when the Center was built.

government as well as recreation and activity rooms, a gymnasium and a day-care facility. Outdoors there are tennis and basketball courts, a playground and parking for now-essential automobiles. Before this facility was built, the Town held its annual meetings at the 4-H Center and had business offices in an outbuilding. Town trucks and other heavy equipment are still garaged there. The Town more recently added a wing to the Center for additional government offices and a town hall for meetings, concerts, art shows, social gatherings, and private events hosted by Town residents.

❖

The Town shares the **Elm Street Urban Park** with the Maryland-National Capital Park and Planning Commission. It is a city block bordered by Elm Street, 46th, 47th and Willow Lane. It has Jenny Read's bronze sculpture "Girl With Hoop" as a centerpiece, and tables and benches where Bethesda office workers can relax on their lunch hour.

The Town dedicated its first park to **Fred and Carl Zimmerman** who had transformed a public strip of land across Maple Street from their house into a spectacular flower garden. The Town took over its maintenance when they moved away. The Town also maintains seasonal plantings at **Tarrytown Park** on **Lynn Drive** and **Rosemary Triangle Park** where Rosemary and Stanford streets come together at Rosemary Circle. The **Millennium Park**, which is Rosemary Circle renamed, has a white oak planted to mark the new millennium.

Seasonal plantings are maintained by various jurisdictions and a variety of park-like locations. Chevy Chase Village has nine parks. Some of them are pocket parks and others are more formal, such as the **Betty English Park** on Brookeville Road. It was named in honor of a resident who was an outstanding member of the Chevy Chase Chapter of the Garden Club of America. The park is maintained by the Chapter. Another park on Brookeville Road, located on a lot formerly occupied by the old Sonnemann's store and then High's store, is now much favored by dog owners.

In Section 3 a community park at **Fulton Street** has a gazebo which doubles as a bandstand for neighborhood parties. **Shepherd Park** (officially **Chevy Chase Park**) in Martin's Additions provides a field for team sports, a playground for younger children, a tennis court and a steep hill for sledding.

Over the years Chevy Chase gardens have become show places and sites for fund-raising parties. One home owner, on Rosemary Street, filled in a swimming pool to create a garden setting for her sculptures. Another resident, on West

Kirke Street, celebrated the successful conclusion of a law suit on behalf of a Pacific Northwest Indian tribe, by carving a totem pole from a tree stump to tell the story. An Anglophile on Raymond Street designed and built a folly of Palladian proportions. Many gardens offer special tree house designs or unique plantings of flowers, shrubs or trees.

In contrast to planned spaces and the urban build-up is the **Capital Crescent Trail,** a popular hiker-biker oasis stretching from Georgetown to Bethesda and on eastward along the northern edge of the Town of Chevy Chase to Rosemary Hills. The Capital Crescent Trail and its **Georgetown Branch** (the unpaved section east of Wisconsin Avenue) is maintained by the Maryland-National Capital Park and Planning Commission, as is the adjacent Elm Street Park. Both park and trail have been enjoyed by residents and visitors in the nearby hotels since 1988.

The Capital Crescent Trail, which follows the B & O train line, offers an escape from traffic along a woodsy path.

Traffic came to Chevy Chase with the completion of I-495, the Capital Beltway, in 1964. Interstate 495 has an exit at Connecticut Avenue which funnels automobiles directly through the "main street" of Chevy Chase. Fortunately for Francis Newland's dream-come-true, the Beltway's route lies in the valley between Chevy Chase and Kensington, and trucks are rerouted to Wisconsin Avenue and Brookeville Road.

The Washington Metropolitan Area Transit Authority, or Metro, opened its first stations on the Red Line in 1976. By 1984 the nearest stations for Chevy Chase, at Friendship

Heights and Bethesda, were in operation. Metro's impact is still being felt. Not only were Chevy Chase residents linked to the city by the newest form of public transportation, but residents from the city were coming to Bethesda and Friendship Heights for business, entertainment and shopping. One of the high-rise buildings at the Bethesda Metro, the one with the distinctive slanted roof-line, is named for Francis G. Newlands.

The fountain on Chevy Chase Circle honors Senator Francis G. Newlands for his many achievements.

The official entrance to Chevy Chase is at the Circle where the District of Columbia meets Maryland. The beautification of the Circle was carried out originally by the Garden Club of America in 1933. In 1992 the Friends of Chevy Chase Circle formed, to make "a more attractive gateway into Washington, D.C." The Friends partnered with the National Park Service to plant 475 azaleas, reseed the lawn and improve the pump system for the fountain. The centerpiece is the Newlands fountain surrounded by shrubs, trees and seasonal flowers maintained by the National Park Service, with support from the Friends.

Names of a few of the early residents of the area, mostly landowners like Jones, Cummings, Walsh and Dunlop, are preserved in street names. Newlands himself is remembered in this way, but not his partners Stellwagen, Sharon or Stewart. The success of Chevy Chase can be attributed to the powerful cooperation of three companies – the Chevy Chase Land Company, the Rock Creek Railway and the Union Trust Bank. One of the remarkable things about Newlands' plan is its durability. The Chevy Chase Land Company is still in existence, and the "home suburb" planned more than a hundred years ago has mellowed and grown without losing the distinctive imprint of its original designer. As Francis Newlands' biographer Albert W. Atwood observed: *Chevy Chase may not live in the past but the past lives in it.*

Francis Newlands' grandchildren William Waring Johnston and Janet Sharon Johnston enjoyed living in Chevy Chase.

Afterword

The Chevy Chase Historical Society is located on the lower level of the Chevy Chase Branch Library (8005 Connecticut Avenue), open to the public at posted hours and otherwise by appointment. Many items are available at the digital archive www.chevychasehistory.org. To contact individual municipalities:

> Chevy Chase Village (301-654-7300)
> www.chevychasevillagemd.gov
>
> Section 3 of the Village of Chevy Chase (301-656-9117)
> www.chevychasesection3.org
>
> The Town of Chevy Chase (301-654-7144)
> www.townofchevychase.org
>
> The Village of Martin's Additions (301-656-4112)
> www.martinsadditions.org
>
> Village of Chevy Chase Section 5 (301-986-5481)
> www.chevychasesection5.org

Acknowledgments

Unless otherwise credited, the images are from the archives of the Chevy Chase Historical Society. Some are being reproduced here for the first time in book form, and we thank the donors for sharing their photographs with us. The staffs of the municipalities, institutions, clubs and churches were very helpful in fleshing out the Chevy Chase story. We know there's more to tell, and we look forward to additions and corrections from our readers.

Our special thanks to Eleanor Ford, Photo Archivist of the Society for many years, who helped select the illustrations and the information for the captions. George Kinter took many rolls of film to bridge gaps in our story. Carol Coffin conducted a search for suitable maps. Former Executive Director Evelyn Gerson prepared the images for publication. Current Executive Director Stephanie Brown, together with Bridget Hartman, Mary Anne Hoffman, Angela Lancaster, Judith Helm Robinson, Mary Sheehan and Danielle Swanson, read and commented on the text. Our thanks to them and to the unnamed but helpful voices at the other end of a telephone call or an e-mail query, and to Richard Marsh and Jack Stickles on the home front.

References and Resources

Atwood, Albert W. *The Romance of Senator Francis G. Newlands and Chevy Chase.* Washington, D.C.: Records of the Columbia Historical Society, 1966-1968.

Beasley, Maurine. *Kate Field and "Kate Field's Washington": 1890-1895.* Washington, D.C.: Records of the Columbia Historical Society, 1973-1974.

Cavicchi, Clare Lise. *Places from the Past: the Tradition of Gardez Bien in Montgomery County, Maryland.* Maryland-National Capital Park and Planning Commission, 2001.

French, Roderick S. *The Chevy Chase Village in the Context of the National Suburban Movement, 1870-1900.* Washington, D.C.: Records of the Columbia Historical Society, 1973-1974.

George, Mary Roselle. *Developer Influence in the Suburbanization of Washington, D.C.: Francis Newlands and Chevy Chase.* MA thesis, University of Maryland, 1989.

Hobbs, Horace P. *Pioneers of the Potowmack.* Ann Arbor, Michigan University Microfilms, 1964.

Lampl, Elizabeth Jo and Kimberly Prothro Williams. *Chevy Chase: a Home Suburb for the Nation's Capital.* Crownsville, Maryland: Maryland Historical Trust Press, 1998.

Linehan, John, ed. *The Town of Chevy Chase: Past and Present.* Town of Chevy Chase, Montgomery County, Maryland, 1990.

Offutt, William. *Bethesda: a Social History.* Bethesda, Maryland: Innovation Game, 1995.

MacMaster, Richard K. and Ray Eldon Hiebert. *A Grateful Remembrance: the Story of Montgomery County, Maryland, 1776-1976.* Rockville, Maryland: Montgomery Country Historical Society, 1976.

Thompson, Robert H., ed. *The Chevy Chase Club, 1892-1992.* Elliott and Clark Publishing, 1992.

Wright, Gwen, William B. Bushong and Clare Lise Cavicchi. *Chevy Chase, Maryland Survey District Survey Report: Phase Two.* Montgomery County Historic Preservation Commission, June 1997.

Index

About the Authors

JOAN MARSH is a founder of the CCHS and for many years her home sheltered the Society collections. She is the author of a biography of *Martha Washington* (Franklin Watts, 1993) and other historic persons. Joan and her husband have lived in the Village of Chevy Chase for sixty years.

FRANCES STICKLES is the author of *A Crown for Henrietta Maria, Maryland's Namesake Queen* (Maryland Historical Press, 1988) among other titles. She and her husband lived forty years in the Town of Chevy Chase. This is a joint effort to showcase the Chevy Chase Historical Society and to encourage the use of its resources.